Polaroids
from the Dead

Also by Douglas Coupland

Polaroids
from the Dead

DOUGLAS
COUPLAND

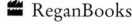 **ReganBooks**
An Imprint of HarperPerennial
A Division of HarperCollins*Publishers*

The following essays first appeared in slightly different form in these publications: "Polaroids from the Dead" in *Spin* (April 1992); "Lions Gate Bridge" (originally titled "This Bridge Is Ours") in *Vancouver Magazine* (March 1994); "The German Reporter" in *Tempo;* "Letter to Kurt Cobain" in *The Washington Post;* "Harolding in West Vancouver" (February 1994), "Postcard from Los Alamos (Acid Canyon)" (February 1994), "Postcard from Palo Alto" (May 1994) and portions of "Brentwood Notebook" (December 1994) in *The New Republic*; "James Rosenquist's F-111" in *Artforum* (April 1994).

A hardcover edition of this book was published in 1996 by ReganBooks, an imprint of HarperCollins Publishers.

HarperCollins books may be purchased for educational, business, or sales promotional use. For information please write: Special Markets Department, HarperCollins Publishers, Inc., 10 East 53rd Street, New York, NY 10022.

First ReganBooks/HarperPerennial edition published 1997.

Designed by Nina Gaskin

The Library of Congress has catalogued the hardcover edition as follows:

Coupland, Douglas.
    Polaroids from the Dead/by Douglas Coupland.—1st ed.
        p. cm.
    ISBN 0-06-039149-9
    1. Grateful Dead (Musical group) 2. Rock music fans. 3. Rock music—Social aspects. 4. Music and society. I. Title.
ML421.G72C68 1996
813'.54—dc20   95-5764
                                                                                                            MN

ISBN 0-06-098721-9 (pbk.)

00 01 ❖/RRD 10 9 8 7 6 5 4 3

Contents

Introduction

KITCHEN DRAWER
FILLED WITH PHOTOS

The pieces in this book reflect an early 1990s worldview that seems time-expired now—jettisoned behind us like sparkling chunks of Apollo rocket tumbling back to earth.

This book—comprised of both fiction and nonfiction—explores the world that existed in the early 1990s, back when the decade was young and had yet to locate its own texture. Back in 1990, North American society seemed to be living in a 1980s hangover and was unclear in its direction. People seemed unsure that the 1990s were even going to be *capable* of generating their own mood. Now I read these pieces over, and it's as though I've opened a kitchen drawer and found a Kleenex box full of already nostalgic Polaroid snapshots and postcards. I hope the photographic imagery in the book will help accentuate this feeling of riffling through evocative old missives.

Anyway, hindsight is twenty-twenty: most people are now more than well aware of vast changes altering everyday life—changes that quickly made the eighties seem as far away from the 1990s as East is from West. Many of these changes, I hope, are reflected in the pieces contained in this book.

It seems important to me to remember that as our world seemingly "accelerates," the expiry dates on "what defines an era" either shrink or become irrelevant. I find myself thinking wistfully of that place in time, say, not three years ago, when teenage bedrooms again sprouted daisy stickers and when Grunge ruled the catwalks. On another level, I think of when the imperative to become "wired" hadn't yet so much filled the world's workforce with dark dreams of low-tech paranoia and security-free obsolescence. It's been a busy half decade.

This book is mainly an examination of people and places I found fascinating (for whatever reasons we develop fascinations) during this brief window in time. My main area of attraction is the milieu in which I and much of North America was raised: middle-middle-class life, and how this middle class underwent, and continues to undergo, a profound transformation. Between 1990 and 1996, ideas once considered out on "the edge" or "the fringe" became the dominant ideas in everyday discourse: the vanishing middle; the collapse of entitlement; the rise and dominance of irony; extreme social upheaval brought about by endless new machines . . . and the sense that even a place in time as recent as last week can now feel like it happened a decade ago.

"Polaroids from the Dead" was "experienced" over a series of Grateful Dead concerts at the Oakland–Alameda County Coliseum the weekend before I turned thirty, in 1991. Since then, of course, the band's leader, Jerry Garcia, has died and the Grateful Dead have disbanded—and the intensely distilled reality they once stood at the center of, has, for the time being, dispersed. I've always been happy with this series of mini-stories, and were I to do them again, the only thing I might change is to convey more clearly the amount of joy the concerts' attendees experienced while there—or just the plain good fun they had.

The stories in Washington, D.C., were researched over a two-week period bridging the Super Tuesday primaries in 1992. In them I tried to capture certain political sentiments of people working inside the political world—and the way people and machines have modified an act as simple as voting.

The "Brentwood Notebook" was written in 1994, months after the Brown Simpson/Goldman murders. It was to have been written a year previously as a municipal analysis similar to the piece on Palo Alto (also in this book). But without a "story hook," I found it pretty well impossible to find a magazine editor interested in running a story on an anonymous, invisible Los Angeles neighborhood. ("But that's the point!" I would explain, "Its invisibility!") I have always found that things become utterly invisible just moments before they explode. The piece was compiled over a period of one day, the thirty-second anniversary of Marilyn Monroe's ambiguous Brentwood death, her house a brisk ten-minute walk from O. J. Simpson's North Rockingham house, just up above Sunset Boulevard. Backup historical information was done over the next few days. The "verdict" has come and gone, but the essential essence of ambiguity and death—the core of the article—remains as true, if not truer, than ever. Brentwood's artifice might not breed or cause the events that happen there, but nevertheless it does create a continually fitting setting for them. It is not intended as any sort of indictment of either Brentwood or Los Angeles but as an attempt to make visible the previously invisible.

Anyway, I'm going on too long here. My finest regards,

Doug

Part One

Polaroids from the Dead

1

THE 1960s ARE DISNEYLAND

AP/Wide World Photos

"Are we in the 1960s yet?" asks Cheyenne.

"Hippies smell like booger," says Amy.

Rain is falling on Oakland for the first time in five years. The drought is over. Scott, Amy, Todd and Cheyenne sit hamstered inside Scott's stepmother's steamy-windowed Lexus, parked atop Spyglass Road, surveying the moistening, months-old remains of the Oakland Hills fire storm—hills once bursting with sequoias, Nile lilies, sago palms and mansions, now all incinerated into a fine oyster-gray dust the color of recycled paper.

"I mean, if the Soviets *really* wanted to roast the Bay Area," says Todd, "they didn't need a bomb. A hibachi and a few drunk teenagers would have been way cheaper."

"Whose picture is that on the acid?" calls Cheyenne from the rear seat, mopping up a gin spill from her Okie dress and Goodwill cardigan.

"Your mother's."

"Fuck *on*, Scott."

"It's Bart Simpson," says Amy, the in-car substance authority. "Eighty mikes. And avoid the peace-sign blotter circulating around now because it's totally washout."

A half-hour previously the four friends had liaisoned in Walnut Creek at the Broadway Plaza Mall, their tribe-defining shopping nucleus. Now, serenaded by a My Dad Is Dead CD, they cruise into Oakland via the Highway 24 tunnel through the Berkeley Hills, all four eager to be punctual for Deadhead–parking lot action at the Oakland–Alameda County Coliseum. Nutty pre-concert fun starts at four o'clock.

Todd spots a melted satellite dish down the hill. "Imagine BMX'ing in this shit. Or using ATVs. Better buy Mom some more scratch-'n'-wins."

"Wasn't she a hippie?" asks Cheyenne.

"Booger-booger-booger," chants Amy. "A sixties chick."

"The 1960s . . ." Todd begins. He considers that era as distant and meaningful to his own life as that of the Civil War or the Flintstones—faint images of beehive hairdos, the moon walk, fat guys with bad haircuts yelling at helicopters. "I don't like the 1960s," Todd decides. "I'd rather be here. Now."

Amy chews apricot leather and scans the cities below, down the gray slopes: Oakland, Alameda, Emeryville, Berkeley—and San Francisco across the Bay—birthplaces of the transuranium elements, flower power, nouvelle cuisine and the Intel microchip. Amy sees these cities now slick with water and cottoned in a fine Pacific mist the ash color of burned houses. She remembers the day last October when the hills ignited—she inventories her mental images of exploding eucalyptus trees, Siamese cats sizzling inside garages-turned-kilns, sparrows burning their claws landing on the stove-element-hot husks of Jeeps, frightened citizens escaping from walls of flame only to drive down the wrong road into fire storms and molten deaths.

*   *   *

And now the hills are cool and damp.

Amy sees a road sign out the window, but the painted letters have burned off. A few minutes ago driving uphill she saw a sign saying, THIS WAS ONCE SOMEONE'S HOME. GO AWAY. Well, she thinks, at least at a Dead concert you can forget for a few hours that the world is going to go *bang*. You pay your money and you hop on the ride: Fun costumes, tunes as seen on MTV, and afterward you can return to the present.

A cop pounds the window.

"Whoa!" A startled Scott lowers the glass. Apparently the Lexus is parked in a potential mud-slide zone; they must drive on. And so they do—down past the now-rusted melted stoves and heating tanks of the ex-mansions, down onto Highway 24, which connects to the once-quake-pancaked Interstate 880 Nimitz Freeway, then toward the Coliseum parking lot, licking their Bart Simpson acid and dodging jackknifed big rigs and liquid oxygen spills along the way, Scott amusing his friends with tales of his hypothetical career working in the used-car lots of Antarctica.

"In the 1960s they had Merry Pranksters," says Cheyenne. "What do we have now?"

"Wacky funsters," answers Scott.

"Look!" says Amy, rolling down her window amid the entranceway gridlock of VW microbuses. "A Tricia Nixon dress—that's *so* cool."

"History is cool," says Todd, nodding.

Scott, Amy, Todd and Cheyenne near the concert. Already the scorched hill behind them has been forgotten, along with the other news of the day—minor temblors in Watsonville and Loma Prieta and controversy over the storage of vasectomized nuclear weapons up-Bay in Richmond. But a smattering of the imagery they have seen today will stick. Their way of looking at the world, continuing a process that began fifteen years ago back in day care, will become even more fortressed.

Scott thinks, as he inches toward the lot, that if he, Amy, Todd and Cheyenne

killed enough old people, or if enough old people were killed, or if enough old people were simply to die, or if the system imploded and the four of them were somehow magically able to afford to build houses of their own, he would design a house for the *real* world. *His* roof would be shingled with slate, not tinderbox cedar, *his* yard would be free of flammable trees-of-death, *his* water would be stored in vast dark black tanks buried deep beneath the soil, and *his* walls, though stuccoed in bright and amusing colors like bubble-gum, lemon or swimming-pool blue, would be lined with steel.

2

YOU ARE
AFRAID
OF
THE SMELL
OF
SHIT

"DEADHEADS AREN'T LIKE DUNGEONS AND DRAGONS FREAKS OR STAR TREKKIES," says Ross, "though there is, of course, some overlap. Don't crush the puppy."

Daniel trips over a bewildered Samoyed pup then looks up to see a grim reaper–costumed figure headed his way carrying a basket of oranges. The puppy sniffs Daniel's nose and darts off; Daniel's jeans are soaked from the lakes of water formed by the downpour of rain. Behind him a waterlogged, gone-to-seed surf dude in bib overalls and a Guatemalan sweater juggles cartons of soy milk and shouts, "Doses! Doses!" Next to him prances a pretty blond girl with dilated pupils in an anorak and a tie-dyed hippie skirt. She blesses all passersby with waves of her wand—a rainbow-striped stick tipped with glistening, frayed silver Mylar filaments.

"God, Ross. The guys here all look like Charles Manson," says Daniel as he rights himself, "and the women all look like Sharon Tate."

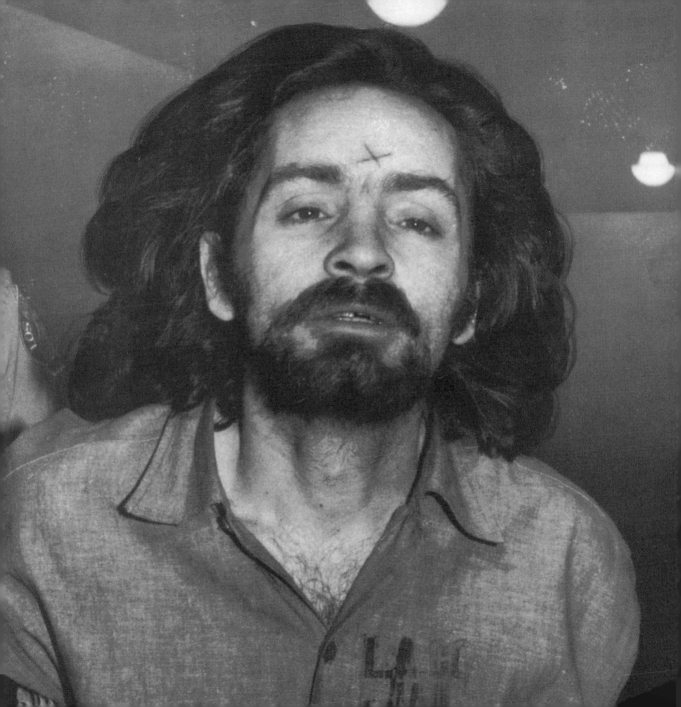

"Certain archetypal dramas continue to replay themselves over and over," replies Ross, who plans to major in philosophy. "Want a carob cookie? And where did Tamara and Stacey go?"

This is Daniel's first Grateful Dead concert. Having seen the freaky skeleton video on MTV, Daniel is curious about the Dead, but not curious to the point of drugging, which might affect his GPA and condemn him to a life batter-frying poultry byproducts in fast-food restaurants. Ross, in his FUCK THA POLICE T-shirt, is Daniel's old high school buddy from San Raphael. Thankfully tolerant of Daniel's nerdiness, Ross can occasionally inflict a graze wound: *"I smell oregano burning. Is Dan nearby?"*

Daniel has heard lore of the Dead pre-concert parking-lot scene, but the actuality of the event is overpowering: a dope-smoke-scented anti-mall, constructed of crammed-together beat-up rustbucket trucks, vans and school buses license-plated mainly from California, Oregon, Washington, B.C., Nevada, Colorado and Arizona. In front of these vehicles, an impromptu tent city of vendors flaunt standard head-shop goodies: antler pipes, skeleton decals, skull candles, tie-dyed shirts, porcupine quills, juggling supplies, Peruvian mittens, conspiracy-theory paperbacks, rolling papers and bumper stickers: MUCHAS GARCIAS and ONE NUCLEAR FAMILY CAN RUIN YOUR WHOLE DAY and JUST SAY N_2O TO DRUGS.

Older hippie ladies ripe with B.O. gorge on condom balloon animals of nitrous oxide; relentless bongo drums beat; troll hippies in plaid flannel shirts vend health food dinners soaked with rain—"Veggie stir-fry! Veggie stir-fry!"

Daniel buys a Styrofoam plate of tofu, hijiki mushrooms, tamari sauce and Maui onion bits. "With lecithin and engevista yeast," the spacey vendor proudly says. Daniel holds his plate and asks for a plastic spoon. The troll druggily cackles back, "Hey, man, I'm or*gan*ic."

Daniel abandons the cutlery-free plate on the vendor's counter next to a mandala-painted sea-salt shaker. He then drifts back to home base for the early evening: Ross's five-color 1971 microbus, which differs from other nearby buses by the driftwood, bungie cords and Kurt Vonnegut novels crammed between the dash and the front window and by a battery-powered space heater glowing from within like a Chernobyl reactor core. A saucily upside-down U.S. flag flaps in the stormy wind above the plastic tarpaulin canopying the VW's sliding doors. Ross says, "Microbuses are the interlocking paving stones of the New Dark Age."

Before entering the van, Daniel avoids a mound of puppy shit lying under the slightly less wet area covered by the tarpaulin. Once inside he suggests to his schoolmates, all UC Berkeley freshmen like himself, and all smoking mystery substances from a bong, that perhaps somebody in the van has trailed a dab of the puppy's business inside.

"Daniel," says Ross, marveling at Daniel's coolness deficiency, "nothing is more bourgeois than fear of the smell of feces. Chill. Swig this." Ross hands Daniel a beer. "Look. There go Tamara and Stacey. Come along, Deadsters."

Farther down the congested and soaking wet medieval midway, Daniel and Ross meet Tamara and Stacey, standing under another tarpaulined space where instant fire logs burn directly on the tar surface of the parking lot. "Greetings, Deadlets," says Ross. "Love the wimple, Stace."

Stacey pats her wimple—a pointy purple velvet Maid Marion hat. "Thanks Ross." She attempts lighting small cones of wisteria- and lotus-scented incense to cover the petroleum reek of burning tar.

"What music are they drumming?" Daniel asks the group.

"Kwakiutl and Haida chants," says Tamara, burrowing into her fanny pack full of pine cones and polished moonstones for a sugar cube, which she finds, then swallows. "Isn't it great?" She offers a cube to Daniel, who awkwardly declines.

The Econoline van next to the fire hosts a 24-inch Hitachi monitor displaying a never-ending spiral of vibrant Mandelbrot fractal patterns. Daniel hears a helium-charged squeaking voice shopping for Ecstasy. Nearby dogs (so many dogs!) gobble discarded grilled-cheese sandwiches and sniff one another's bums, remembering each other from Dead shows in Meadowlands, Nassau and Shoreline.

Emerson and Dale—friends of Ross—discuss the evening's possible lineup of songs with a curatorial facility Daniel had considered to be held only by his mother's wine-bore boyfriends. "No, *no*. They opened the second set of the first

1989 Spectrum show in Philadelphia with 'China Cat Sunflower,' not 'One More Saturday Night.'"

Stacey, thrilled to be moist, stands outside the tarpaulin and stares at the darkening sky and the rain along with a clique of other kids clad in Glad bags, fringed buckskin coats, Aztec ponchos, Cowichan sweaters and blond dreadlocks tucked within toques and rasta hair cozies. "I feel like one of those sixties photographs," she says. "Are we going inside soon?"

"Right now," says Ross, "Dead ho! That means you, too, Daniel. Having fun?"

Daniel, Ross, Tamara, Stacey, Emerson, Dale and others in their group enter the damp and snaking throng of line into the coliseum. How young the crowd looks, Daniel thinks. Why there's almost nobody over twenty-two in the entire parking lot. This thought surprises him, because he had always believed the Dead were for clapped-out old hippies and bikers. He mentions this abundance of youth to Ross, who replies by saying, "Look at those two old coots there."

"Where?"

"The fiftysomethings over by the pylons. Man, they must be doing pretty wild stuff over there. Look how into it they are. I'm curious—I'm gonna go check what they're doing."

Ross scampers over to the two older, bearded men—1960s survivors indulging in a small, manually complicated ritual—and asks a question or two, then scampers back to his friends in line. Asks Tamara, "What were they doing?"

Ross replies, disgusted, "Contact lenses."

3

YOU ARE
EXHAUSTED
BY
RISK

"HITLERBERRIES."

"Huh?"

"Hitlerberries." Caroline plucks a frilled strawberry hull from a ripe berry, depositing it into her backpack. She then eats the berry. "Ever notice how there aren't any deformed strawberries these days? Remember how there used to be deformed—*weak*—berries hidden in the bottoms of the baskets? Now they're all perfect. Boring. Flavorless."

Mario only half pays attention. He is hypnotized by a new bleeding tattoo of the sun on Caroline's left calf. This is a tattoo garnered not thirty minutes previously in the parking lot in the rear of a gutted, Oregon-plated Chevy station wagon latex-painted with violet Jolly Roger skull and crossbones.

Caroline and Mario are seated fourteen rows up, directly opposite the stage—choice seats—waiting for the show to begin and watching oval pink balloons the

Michael Zelner

size of pigs being batted about by the audience. They inhale from the Coliseum's syrupy microclimate. This is sweet druggy air, which only two months ago Caroline, a child of the Silicon Valley, might have feared was a breeding ground for multidrug-resistant tuberculosis, but this is air which she now positively vacuums in with abandon, enthralled to catch a wave of patchouli oil or vegetarian sweat, the air humid from so much evaporating clothing.

Caroline's hair is woven into thin corn rows—the proto-dreadlock phase. Just prior to her tattoo she had breezily informed Mario that she had skipped a period. When they connected three months ago, *he* was the cooler member of the relationship.

"And for that matter," Caroline continues, back on her theme of strawberries and eugenics, "there aren't deformed babies born anymore. Ever notice? All aborted, I guess. Imagine a world without midgets. Do you ever worry about biotechnology?"

"Uh—" Mario stalls. He doesn't understand half of what Caroline says these days. Somewhere, about two weeks back, Mario guesses, they crossed the point where it was mutually assumed *he* was smarter, or rather Caroline stopped pretending that he was. Maybe it was the exam hell or maybe it was the mescaline. Caroline's current looseness is shocking compared to her previous uptight self, when she was like one of those ladies in cherry blazers who work behind the airline counters.

"Life is so serious," Caroline had told Mario when they first met at Katie's garage sale. "One screwup and you're doomed. I honestly think the world is a harsher place now than when my mother was a hippie back in the sixties. The stakes are so unimaginable now." Her uptightness had made her seem vulnerable—attractive. Now, it is as though she is exhausted by the future, by options. Exhausted by risk. Yesterday she threw away all her makeup.

"Do you—" starts Caroline, but Mario interrupts her. "Hey, I like your tattoo."

Caroline, seemingly already having forgotten her new marking, looks at her calf. "Oh, yeah. Skin. Sometimes I wish I was a skeleton. No skin. So I didn't have to feel like an object."

Well. So much for chitchat, thinks Mario. They lean back and absorb the crowd scene and listen to drum noises. Mario caresses the limp crown of American Beauty roses woven around Caroline's skull. He goes to the bathroom and scores four tabs of 100-microgram acid from a Santa Barbara skater dude, $3 apiece. On the blotter paper are images of open windows.

Mario returns to his seat, and Caroline resumes her discussion about science.

"Aw, Caroline," pleads Mario, "the show's gonna start in a second. Can we discuss stuff later?"

"No, Mario, this is important. Don't you ever wonder about the way the world is going? This weird global McNugget culture we live in? All our ideas and objects and activities being made of fake materials ground up and reshaped into precisely measurable units entered into some rich guy's software spreadsheet program?"

Mario stares blankly at Caroline.

"I'm not going to shave my armpits anymore, Mario. Look at us. Long hair, but it's squeaky clean. Bare feet, sure, but your dad's Prelude is waiting for us outside. It's so hypocritical."

"Your life, baby."

The band comes onstage and the crowd roars. Mario hands Caroline two tabs. "Cheer up, baby. Come on. Embrace the meltdown." Then, pleased with himself for catching the drift of her lecture, he adds, "We're the McDead."

"Yes," says Caroline, placing the open windows inside her body, dreaming of another world where complex issues refuse to masquerade as oversimplicities, "we're the McDead."

4

T OR F:
SELF-PERFECTION
IS ATTAINABLE
WITHIN
YOUR
LIFETIME

FETUS AND THE PHOENICIAN PHOENECIAN ARE PURCHASING ORANGE DRINKS FROM A concession stand.

"It's not a *uni*verse," shouts the Phoenician Phoenecian above the blare of tunage flowing in from the concert, "it's a *multi*verse."

"Wow, man," mumbles Fetus, cartoonishly, groggily, his white goatee dipping into his drink.

The Phoenician Phoenician, a.k.a. Dennis, is a freelance data-entry worker from Mill Valley, born in Phoenix, Arizona, who was informed by a long-departed girlfriend, Rhianna, that he was once a healer in ancient Phoenecia.

Fetus is Carl, so named for his tendency to regress while on drugs.

The two friends have been following the Dead for two decades, and neither is edgy at the thought of missing a few minutes of show. Besides, Dennis wants to start his Yueh-Ling twirl dancing now, and Fetus, well, Fetus just wants to go get fetal with the waste cases in the seats out behind the stage.

"Later, bro'," says Fetus, backing away from Dennis, flashing a peace sign. Fetus then stumbles over a plump baby crawling after a blue Citibank balloon, causing Fetus to slop his orange drink. He regains his balance, smiles with relief, flashes a peace sign at the baby's mother, then bumps backward into a Deadhead in a Eureka Loggers football T-shirt who is using a Pacific Bell booth, causing Fetus's orange drink to fall splat onto the cement of the concourse.

"Oh, wow—" he editorializes, "gravity really *works*," and he is off into the arena.

Dennis laughs at his friend. Fetus is so . . . *human*, Dennis thinks with a slight note of reprobation. He wishes Fetus would work on himself more. Dennis is ninety-nine percent *there*, he believes. He has the rest of his life to polish up the remaining one percent—toddle off to Big Sur . . . check out the sunrises in Solano County . . . learn to speak Dolphin.

"Shoes off!" Dennis says to himself and hurls away the shackles of corporate domination. To the pulse of the music, and along with hundreds of other spinning dancers in the corridors, Dennis commences freedom dancing, his mouse-brown dreadlocks atwirl, red cotton drawstring pants and elfin red beard flowing with the guitars and drumspace of the Dead, all the while avoiding occasional blots of lentil-enhanced barf and foil sprinklings of pixie dust.

During the next song break Dennis gulps his orange drink. A young Deadhead asks him if he can score a dose. "If you have to ask to buy it, then you won't be able to deal with it," Dennis replies, with what he hopes is gravity.

"Cry into your dime bag, you hippie weed," replies the youngster.

Really. These kids. Shows weren't always like this, Dennis thinks, vaguely angry and perplexed as he resumes his spinning-dance routine. Dead shows were the same as always until, *kablooey*, the MTV video happened and the kiddies began showing up, eager to party, not appreciating the true Dead spirit. *Some* of the new kiddies don't even bother participating in the complex, rule-packed ritual of mailing away for concert tickets, showing up only for a groove in the parking lot.

Well, at least Dennis has an audience. At least he can transmit the Yueh-Ling organic dance lore on to a new generation of twirlers and spinners—a master passing his craft to new generations. He can become . . . wait . . . over by the T-shirt booth . . . that tender young Deadling in the prairie dress. Is she, or is she not mimicking Dennis's dance moves? Why, she could become Dennis's new . . . *disciple*. Yes.

HAIR WRAPS
Lovingly crafted with
Beads & Bells & many different colors

5

TINKERING
WITH
OBLIVION
CARRIES
RISKS

Dave Weiland

DOYLE, CLAD IN HAPHAZARD LAYERS OF LONG JOHNS, GYM PANTS, SECONDHAND sweaters, ribbed work socks and boots, lumbers through the fluorescent-lit spinning mob in the hallways. *Fake Deadheads*, he thinks. *Fake Deadheads*. He wishes they would all spontaneously combust.

Head hunched under his brown felt fedora, Doyle scowls at the youngsters. His head jitters back and forth, continually on the alert for either Masonic imagery or a glimpse of Thomas Pynchon. He wonders if one of these kids would enjoy sifting through a leaflet promoting the denazification of Humboldt County.

These foolish modern TV kids, asleep in a galaxy of pornographic beer commercials and anti-drug hysteria. They think their own personal choice of obliteration defines them as individuals: what brand of beer they piss, what species of toad they lick. But they are wrong. *Obliteration* will define *them*, and not the other way around. These kids wouldn't know a bad trip if it shat on them: freight trains bleeding dead birds; Kodiak bears dipping live dolphins and their own paws into a McDonald's deep fryer; celestial imagery feeding on itself; diarrhea like a steel pipe impaled in their rectums.

Doyle tramps down the rampways, onto the floor, out to the standing worms of microphones being held aloft by the "tapers": Dead fans taping the evening's show. *Fools*, thinks Doyle, *fools*. Even his own peers don't recognize the fragility of the Dead scene. Cops videotape the parking lots; skull stickers are probable cause for vehicle inspection in New Jersey; tour rats feed acid to puppies; Dead women squat to pee on park lawns.

Doyle's reverie is snapped when an Oakland Coliseum staff person tells him to either keep moving or stay within the white crowd control lines.

Fascists, thinks Doyle, *fascists* . . .

6

YOU
DON'T
OWN
YOUR
BODY

DIANA IS VISITING OAKLAND, CALIFORNIA, FROM HAWAII WHERE SHE DEVELOPS REAL estate on the Big Island. Tonight's concert intermission is nearly over, and Diana has returned to the arena's floor after inspecting her two children down in the nursery—Jesse and Hope—and ensuring that their foam earplugs are fully taped in place and that the vibes are good. Cody, Diana's husband, is up in the stands. He's chatting with an old friend, Keith, about the DEA's new heat-seeking radar copters being deployed to ferret out dope plantations in Siskiyou County. Keith's okay—as long as he keeps on that lithium carbonate. All in all, the night is shaping up well.

Diana feels sexy this evening. She's wearing her black Neiman Marcus cocktail dress with emu-skin cowboy boots and around her neck a Zuni leather pouch stuffed with runes and quartz crystals. Diana feels older tonight, too, much older than the young children who vastly outnumber her here at the concert. She feels a wave of affection for these Junior Deadheads and yet sorry for them too. She feels that useful truths have been abandoned over the past years, that modern young people aren't being taught the right words to ask the right questions.

But Diana is happy that tonight the girls are going without makeup and bras. The world is *about* women being beautiful; the world is *about* people just being people. Diana likes the idea of her own fuzzy armpits above her strapless dress shocking some of the younger boys at the show—the suburban mall boys who don't even know that women sprout hairs there. She likes the idea of her body being 100 percent owned by herself—like real estate. It worries Diana how naïvely people surrender ownership of their bodies to others—spouses, the state, the church, big science—all the while falsely thinking they have control over their own flesh: clitorectomy, bride burning, circumcision, veils, GI haircuts, all reproductive technologies . . . biology under siege. So many people willing—and eager—to tell *you* what to do with your body, what *you* should feel shameful about. Anorexia, bulimia, Nautilus, Barbie dolls and the application of Nair . . . the list seems endless to Diana.

Even the ownership of minds is tenuous nowadays, Diana is beginning to think. Two days ago in Hawaii, young Jesse was simultaneously playing Tetris, watching *Doogie Howser*, humming along to Kriss Kross, all the while talking to Charlie next door over the headset unit that resembles those worn by CAA agents in Beverly Hills. Jesse became a living computer screen with multiple windows—information flowing and channeling effortlessly from window to window. The incident made Diana wonder if people are reverting back to the soundless communication state of animals, speaking a new language of pie charts, mouse clicks and bar codes. Not the world she has once envisioned.

Cody returns just as the music starts and a tab of acid kicks in with a colorful, sparkling wash. "Hey, feeling good, honey?" he asks.

"Like Las *Vegas*," she replies with a wink.

The lights dim; the crowd roars. Diana imagines a helicopter landing on her front yard in Hawaii, the blades blasting away the Fisher Price toys that litter the

Dave Weiland

grass. She imagines Hawaiian state troopers stepping out from the helicopter and warning her of lava flowing down the slope toward her house from the lake of magma high up the mountain. And then she sees the lava river itself, not a base-ball throw away, its blackened marshmallow-crust slime now encircling a plume-ria tree, the tree's sap spitting like hamburgers on a barbecue grill.

Diana watches fingers of the lava approach her house, nudging around the red-wood siding, bending the aluminum laundry-room door, breaking the door down, the lava filling up the kitchen, making tins of pineapple and jars of preserved cher-ries burst and cook, making scalding hot water explode from the showers and boil in the toilets.

Diana watches Cody's satellite dish and her Caprice Classic carried down the slope. And she follows the lava stream down to the ocean—black crackling may-onnaise, its surface popping and crackling like . . . like . . . Polaroid flashbulbs, no, like Bic lighters popping at a concert.

And then the lava hits the turquoise ocean water and crumbles in shock as it hardens, disintegrating, forming a new beach of warm black sand—a beach which Diana now owns and over which she now runs. *This* is a beach that lies in a place where no beach ought to be. Wave patterns will soon lick that black sand away. And this is a beach which, after being washed away in the night, will never be walked on again.

7

YOU
FEAR
INVOLUNTARY
SEDATION

SPECK WAS INITIALLY ATTRACTED TO THE STATE OF FLORIDA BECAUSE THE STATE itself is shaped like a handgun. That was four years ago. After that he drifted. In Texas he worked as a diet cop for a TV talk-show host, spending endless sojourns in restaurants making sure that only salads were ordered, that only Sweet'n Low sweetened. In Arizona he learned how to fix air conditioners but thought he'd develop mental illness from the tedium. After that he drifted back up to his hometown of Dearborn, Michigan—"the Silicon Valley of 1947"—but winter cold reminded Speck of why he'd left in the first place.

During a pit stop in Berkeley, Speck hooked up with a Northern California spinster he met, mundanely, in the produce section of Andronico's, the gourmet grocery store that sells eighteen different hybrids of apple. Alice—fortysomething and the heiress to a Stockton rice dynasty—was of the same pinafore-wearing mold as Miss Jane Hathaway of *The Beverly Hillbillies.* Alice bought Speck a pair of barbells and a red telephone shaped like a Porsche; Speck sleeps in his own room downstairs and, once a week, in hers.

Tonight Speck is at a Grateful Dead concert at the Oakland–Alameda County Coliseum, having Jonesed himself a miracle ticket out in the parking lot. Alice thinks he is at his AA meeting, a group she obliquely refers to as "the Temperance League." Alice herself is out tonight, too, at a university-sponsored literary do. Speck doesn't really know *what* the do is about; he doesn't pay too close attention to Alice's day-to-day life; she's so square and so easily fooled. Speck wishes Alice would surprise him a bit more. He tries, however, not to be gratuitously cruel with her; between them exists a pleasing silence. Sometimes Speck feels as though Alice has mailed him a letter and that she doesn't want to waste words talking until the letter arrives and he has read it. So Speck is curious. And besides—Alice's shingled Arts and Crafts house on Hearst Avenue is too comfortable. He has promised himself he will *not* steal the tiny Miró landscape in the living room.

    Just into the band's second set, while rinsing from his face a film of concert dope smoke, Speck can see under the Coliseum's harsh bathroom lighting that his looks are fading quickly. The bloom is off. Today is his twenty-fifth birthday. His freshness is being replaced with a hardness. Speck, a tough critic of bodies, can see his tightening facial structure making him now appear sullen, possibly oversexed, worst of all, possessing a *past.* Speck figures that although he'll still be able to coast on his appearance, the calculated boyish insouciance that carried him to twenty-five will no longer be viable.

Earlier on that same day, Alice took Speck for a birthday lunch at Chez Panisse on Shattuck Avenue. "The Cheese Penis," she called it at lunch—the dirtiest words Speck had ever heard Alice speak in public. Speck, hard to shock, was shocked. In attendance for the meal were two of Alice's heavy-sweatered 300-IQ friends, Isabel and Lorraine. Main subjects of conversation were changes in the

global weather patterns and the separation of church and state ("Sunday shopping—is that *it*?" asked Alice).

Alice, Isabel and Lorraine seemed to enjoy Speck's comments, and *he*
enjoyed being appreciated for his mind. He told them of his theory of how the
world seems to be running out of animals now, just about the same time Detroit
has run out of animal names for new car models. "A coincidence?" he asked to a
flutter of indulgent titters.

He then mentioned the places he thought would be the worst in which to live
when the oil runs out completely: Honolulu, New England, the Canadian
Maritimes. He mentioned the worst place to live when the electricity stops: the
Sun Belt with all those air conditioners. And he mentioned the worst place to live
when the weather finally collapses: "Just about anywhere except the Pacific
Northwest."

Isabel and Lorraine tried to stroke Speck's ego, make him feel more dangerous—and feed Alice's rough-trade fantasy. Speck loved the attention. He
informed the table of his idea for custom license plates for the Mazda Miata Alice
sometimes talks about: his blood type, ORH-. "So that when I crash," he said, "the
paramedics won't lose any time trying to type my blood." Isabel and Lorraine's
feigned shock made Alice blush gratifyingly. Or maybe the table's giddiness was
a result of ions in the air from the rain. Alice looks out the window; such a rainy
day. The drought of years is over.

Tonight, roaming the bleary, enthusiastic mob at the Grateful Dead concert, Speck
is glad to be in a more hip place with hipper people. He now seeks out what he
has come to find: a blond Samoyed-eyed seventeen-year-old nubeling in need of
spiritual guidance and a post-concert escort to the BART station.

These Dead shows. They used to be a drag when he attended them in his
teens—Hell's Angels and scraggly hippie types. But recently, with the invasion of
the MTV kids, concerts are more like those Woodstock photos he's seen—peace,
love and understanding—except everybody's had a bath now. So many lovely
young things.

But Speck could do without all the skeletons that permeate the concert's environment—skeletons on T-shirts, skeletons on stickers, skeletons on hats and jewelry. The skeletons remind him of a set of Huron Indian bones wired together back home in Michigan—in Ypsilanti near Dearborn—in a waiting room he once inhabited for endless after-school hours as a child while his father cleaned a medical-dental complex.

Maybe if he understood the significance of all these skeletons, Speck could connect with the evening's abundant crop of clear-skinned young girls—girls for whom sex hasn't yet been converted into a series of mechanical, non-procreative collisions. Speck sure needs help tonight—for whatever reason, connections just aren't happening. He wonders if the stress from seeing his aging face in the mirror has psyched him out and made him start to transmit bad vibes to strangers. He must seem so *used-up* to these girls with their fuzz-cheeked boytoys. He must seem terrifying to these youngsters, the way the hippie survivors and casualties with the shrunken apple-head faces who punctuate tonight's concert seem terrifying to him. Or even worse, maybe Speck himself is projecting that same brutal scariness, like those gristled leathery bachelors and stewardesses he sees in the gyms and the airport bars—the straw-permed sex androids from Planet 1971—a Marina del Rey limbo where the postcoital omelettes and mushroom soup stopped a decade ago.

Speck decides to pack in the nubes for the night. He strolls out onto the floor, out past the annoying twirling Deadheads, cursing, "Hey, buddy—it's all fun and games until someone loses an eye."

He strolls down the side aisles, and then he sees *her*—gyrating in her pinafore and singing with her eyes closed, a rope of pearls clacking sideways—it's Alice. Speck freeze-frames; Alice's body is languid and flowing. She is no longer a wobbling spinster but a vision of something fine.

Speck unlocks; he doesn't say hello. Instead he races out to the parking lot and fetches his pickup and speeds up the 880 to Berkeley, to the University off-ramp and up the hill, up to the house on Hearst.

There, he enters his downstairs room, appreciating the silence, deriving extra pleasure from knowing the concert continues at that very moment.

He sits on his bed. Alice has lit a large rainbow-layered candle, which awaits him there on his Shaker side table. "You wingy California chick," he says to himself.

Rain falls on the panes of his window. He can hear himself breathing. For the first time he notices the size of a grandfather sugar pine growing outside his window. He walks across the room, straightens out his barbells, then returns to his bed. He leans over his side table and warms his hands over Alice's candle. "Hey," he says, "I think I'll stay here awhile."

8

YOU CAN'T
REMEMBER
WHAT YOU
CHOSE
TO
FORGET

SOFTWARE HAS RAINED MONEY ON BEN. HE HAS AMASSED A CALIFORNIA FORTUNE that hums like crickets on Ronald Reagan's ranch on a hot summer day. Thank you, Bendix. Thank you, Morton Thiokol. Thank you, GE, Bechtel, Raytheon, Amana, Honeywell and Motorola.

Ben can even forget about the pair of $650 Bally Suisse brogues ruined waiting in line for tonight's concert, shoes he purchased just this afternoon in San Francisco after sifting through his T-bills in the Bank of America VIP vault. He should have known better. Last night, flying in from Boston, the pilot had asked the passengers to pray for rain—an odd intrusion of the mystical world into the secular. The pilot said that a storm dallying off the coast was trying to make up its mind whether to swing inland.

Because of the rain and his wet shoes, Ben can now de-sock with the rest of

the Deadheads without feeling guilty—guilty that his wealth precludes his con-
tinued membership in the sixties culture of his youth, an era he now views
through an AT&T commercial soft-focus lens: a mutt puppy chewing Crazy
Susan's shawl outside the Avalon Ballroom; sunsets over Daly City viewed from
San Bruno, with microdot-freak chatter inside the bus sounding like Charlie
Brown's teachers; nibbling daisy petals in mellow Leandra's polished redwood
Edwardian Kleenex box of a house in Menlo Park; getting naked on Muir Beach.

Dead concerts. Without them, the sixties would be extinct. Ben has used his
money to follow the Dead around the world over the past years: Cairo, Dijon,
Lille, Boulder, Rotterdam . . . pursuing that era, refusing it permission to die.

Ben remembers an old science-fiction movie he once saw, *Silent Running*,
in which Earth had been been nuked and a spaceship—an ark—loaded with
seeds and trees, traveled the universe in search of a new planet to call home.
Oakland–Alameda County Coliseum tonight feels like that spacecraft—the 1960s
being the dead planet and the young Deads, the seeds.

Ben scans the freaks. Koo-koo survivors. Casualties. Ben doesn't consider
himself a casualty, but he knows a fraction of his linear thinking capacity has been
lost because of his tripping. But maybe nonlinearity has helped him with his
defense-related computer work. Ben's daughter, Skye, says he's a spaz. "You
can't be your age, go to Dead shows and *not* be a broken person," she says.
Nineties children are so hard.

Ben, like most of the older Deadheads at tonight's concert, is wearing a gen-
uine article of 1960s culture, a T-shirt saying HELLO SAN FRANCISCO—PLEASE IDEN-
TIFY YOURSELF. No need for anybody here to know he has bank accounts in
Luxembourg.

Skye says hippies dress randomly, like drifters or bag people. "Scary. If you
have to wear that sixties hippie shit, coordinate it, *please*." Skye's own neo-sixties
fashion theories of calculated randomness purchased from the local mall seem to
have strayed from the true essence of hippie couture.

"The sixties were about who you *were*," Ben told Skye, "not about what you looked like."

"Take a bath, Dad."

At the suggestion she attend tonight's show, Skye rolled her eyes and plunked a new Pet Shop Boys CD into her CD-Man, then elevatored down to the Mark Hopkins lobby in search of celebrities. So instead, Ben attended the concert with Allan, an old pal from the Fillmore West era now working as a vascular surgeon in Millbrae. Allan left at halftime: "Great show, Ben. Have to split, though— replacing an alcoholic's veins in the morning. Call you soon."

Sigh. Even the bikers are gone these days, and Skye was right—the aging holdouts are starting to look like cartoonified versions of themselves—Freak Brother-esque beards and vests and denims; Mansonian love-god pantaloons with tattoos and rainbow-wear. "Dead Shows are like a theme park, Dad," Skye says. "GroovyWorld."

And everybody's so poor these days, too. It was so popular for decades to bash the middle class and then suddenly, *pffft*, the middle class evaporated, and now Ben misses it dreadfully. Nonethe*less*, just because other people are poor doesn't mean one shouldn't try to hang on to one's *own* wealth. Let's be sensible. Ben gives to panhandlers, even though they seem more like moochers these days. Just when and how did the world become so polarized?

Another sigh. Dope, not acid for Ben this evening, and not much dope at that. A triangle call with Dresdner Bank is scheduled tomorrow at 6:30 A.M. plus an interview with Skye's teachers at 8:00 P.M. back in Massachusetts.

A lonely gulp of cola.

Strange how when you're young you have no memories. Then one day you wake up and, *boom*, memories overpower all else in your life, forever making the present moment seem sad and unable to compete with a glorious past that now has a life of its own.

Skye says, "Dad, you always complain people my age never protest about anything, but the first moment we even try to make a peep, you ex-hippies are the first to slam us, saying we're nowhere near as passionate or effective as *you* were in those fucking sixties. Make up your minds. Stop making us have to subsidize *your* disillusionment with the way *you* turned out."

Ouch.

Ben reclines and watches galaxial splashings of Bic lighters span the darkened Coliseum's seats. He knows the music will be ending soon. And he wonders—with fear and confusion and a sense of loss—about the alien planet on which tonight's spaceship will be landing.

9

TECHNOLOGY WILL SPARE US THE TEDIUM OF REPEATING HISTORY

Erik and Jamie were going to go swimming tonight, then head to Leon's house for coffee where the suitably postmodern theme for the evening was to be "Commercials We Hate and the People Who Love Them." Jamie was going do her imitation of Suzanne Sommers using a ThighMaster, and Erik his impersonation of Ann B. Davis selling Minute Rice. But just as they were headed out the door, Sherrilyn, "the Krazy Hippie Broad from 2-B," ran up the stairway, handed Jamie two Grateful Dead tickets, gibbered, "A miracle is yours," then charged off, peeling down Bancroft Way in her Celica to visit her mother at the Blue Cross hospital in Sacramento.

"Why not?" they said, dashing back inside for a costume change, hoping to construct an appropriately Summer-of-Love getup, eventually cobbling together a slightly oversanitized and possibly "too Gappy" version of drugged hippie abandon: 501s, desert boots, beat-up sweatshirts, baggy sweaters and, of course, love beads.

That was hours ago. Now the concert is nearly over, and Erik and Jamie are fleeing the Oakland–Alameda County Coliseum a few songs before the show ends.

"I grew up thinking hippies would destroy the world," Erik says. "And I still do."

Jamie adds, after a pause, "Well . . . at least the place was mercifully free of mimes."

The two dash through the parking lot's rainy darkness, past the cold, moist Deahheads who didn't receive the miracle of free tickets and who still party forlornly, out to Elvis, the 1975 Pacer with the Switzerland-clean interior that Jamie bought for $900 last summer.

"You didn't *eat* anything back there, did you, Jamie?" asks Erik, opening the door. "Those people stick acid in *every*thing. I don't want you jumping out the window, thinking you can fly."

Jamie says, "I felt like Andy Warhol in there—when he'd visit Fire Island with speed freaks in the sixties, eating only candy bars and soda pop so he wouldn't get dosed." She changes the subject. "Does anybody make laptop microwave ovens? We could have brought Lean Cuisines."

The car starts.

"Put in a tape. Quick," pleads Jamie.

"Which tape?"

"Songs about robots—written by cash registers. *Anything* to counteract that hippie noise."

New Order saturates the warming car. Erik and Jamie have returned to a future they can live with: spare, secular, coherent and rational—a future reflecting their almost puritanical belief that excess is its own punishment.

Yet while Erik and Jamie are relieved to return to a familiar world, and all too ready to tease the world they have recently vacated, they are also feeling a sense of being let down—as though, however accidentally Erik and Jamie might have arrived at the Coliseum, tonight's concert offered a promise that was not delivered. They had presupposed that such a radically different Deadhead way of life would offer constructive new hints on how to deal with the new thought-based economy the world is plunging toward. It didn't.

"And, Jesus, what's with all those skeletons those people worship, anyway?" asks Erik rhetorically. To Erik, skeletons equal death: first strikes; X rays; rot; Biafra; poisoned milk. "Bloody creepy. Nothing cute or lovable about them. Brrrr . . ." The only positive image of skeletons Erik can conjure is an old David Bowie song, "Chant of the Ever-Circling Skeletal Family," a quirky bit of padding from the *Diamond Dogs* album—an essentially wordless song that evokes in Erik's head images of jets filled with skeletons forever circling the world. Erik tells this to Jamie; he analogizes the image of skeletons riding in planes to vaccines: "Glossy protein shells—the jet's metal body—filled with dead core ribonucleic acid—skeletons inside." Erik's superstition is that as long as 747s circle Earth, humanity remains immune to an unknown scourge that would cast it back into the mud.

"You know what tonight reminded me of?" asks Jamie. "That cartoon we saw in grade school—of a modern nuclear family trapped back in prehistoric time that befriends a caveman family. One week the cave family would learn about, say, toasters and then the next week the teenage cavegirl would learn about, say, dating. It's like, Deadheads aren't from *now*—they're from someplace else—they're that cave family. They're just improvising with whatever's lying around here— school buses et cetera, waiting until they die. They have no commitment to where and when they are, to the society we live in."

Erik shoots back: "You're just projecting your worry about eroding social commitment in general."

"I guess."

The car pulls out of the lot, past Deadheads holding cardboards begging for rides to faraway places: to Wisconsin, to Kamloops, to Morristown. "Sorry, guys," says Erik. They wait at the red stoplight.

"I bet," says Jamie, "if we did acid, we could understand what Deadheads are all about."

"Hey, babe—you go first. And write me a postcard and tell me what it's like."

"No, *you* go first."

"No, *you* go first."

"No, *you* go first."

"No, *you* go first."

The light turns green and Jamie drives on, turning left heading toward the 880 on-ramp. The car windows have steamed up. Erik wipes his window with his sweater and sees a bright light up in the sky over to the left. He rolls down the window a fraction and focuses on the light's source. There to the west over an Oakland industrial park, ascending the sky above the Unisys tower, what he had thought was the moon is a jet.

10

HOW
CLEAR
IS
YOUR
VISION
OF
HEAVEN?

THE BABIES ARE STARING AT THE RAIN.

Columbia, clutching her three-week-old Logan to her breast, says, "Come on, Luke. Shasta honey—inside now," but the twins dawdle outside the 1971 Econoline van's rusted doors, tentatively splashing their chubby toes in cold puddles. California babies, at the age of four they have lived through dust storms and a hundred salty fogs but have never seen a true rain.

Columbia lugs her children up into the van and places them on their foam pads next to the resting German shepherds, Kashmir and Vanilla. Columbia is confused by their fascination. Rain is something that is just, well, *there*—it's not something you're supposed to remember seeing for a first time, like a dead body or a house on fire. She wonders if her children's infatuation with the novelty of rain indicates a mistake she's somehow made in raising them.

Anyway, Columbia is also preoccupied as she undresses her children, preparing them for the rumbling sleep-inducing drive back over the mountains later that night. While she has enjoyed her evening hanging out amid the parking lot scene and chatting with the Deadheads who rambled past the van, she's angry with her husband, Ezekiel. She's not mad at him for leaving her out in the parking lot with the children while *he* attended the concert—three weeks old is simply too young for a baby to attend a concert. Instead Columbia is angry with Ezekiel because of his neglectful behavior back at their house, at their small redwood-shingled geodesic dome in the Sierras of Lassen County.

"Bundle up, sweetie," she tells Luke. "We're heading home soon."

"Back to our house?" asks Luke.

"Yes," Columbia says, placing the baby, Logan, on the passenger seat. "Back to the dome." She helps button on the older children's bedclothes: men's flannel shirts bought for twenty-nine cents apiece at St. Vincent's Thrift Shop in Reno. She rights a tipped-over canister of rice, then sweeps the spillage through a rust hole in the floor.

Yes, she is angry with Ezekiel—Ezekiel had rented a children's plastic swimming pool in Susanville for Logan's wet-birthing. Not that Logan's birth hadn't gone well, mind you—almost deliciously painless, with Logan weighing almost twice as much as Luke and Shasta had combined. Rather, the problem is that Ezekiel never bothered to empty out the swimming pool of the afterbirth and water. The mixture has been sitting in the swimming pool outside the dome, day in, day out, for weeks, evolving into a bizarre dead playboy's layered cocktail—a rusty tomato aspic topped with a pissy yellow vinegar solution. Columbia is disgusted thinking of drought-parched bears and wolves and eagles up in the mountains sipping her fluids; Ezekiel, on the other hand, is aroused by the thought. Columbia is unable to make Ezekiel's mental leap from abomination to mythic sensuality.

When Ezekiel emerges from the concert, which ought to be soon, at least he'd be too out of it to continue the terse mood that had marked their drive from northwest California through the Highway 24 tunnel into Oakland earlier today. Columbia is, she supposes, being uptight. But *really*. And those poor people in Susanville must want their rented swimming pool back soon. And *where* will the money come from to pay them? And when is it ever going to be cleaned?

The twins jiggle sweetly under their quilts, and Kashmir and Vanilla snuffle up against them providing warmth. Circling the children's necks are purple neon glow-strip necklaces made of plastic given to them by Ezekiel's tree-planting partner, Pete, before the show.

The children are tired and a touch edgy. The drumming of rain on the van's steel roof is enervating them. They want a story. Columbia, atop her stool propped next to the doors, and peering out the tiny windows that face the Coliseum far in the distance, tries to improvise, thinking of the stories her mother told *her*, growing up in the commune in Mendocino. She thinks of her world. She sweeps a streak of dirty hair away from her young brow.

"Once upon a time," she begins, "there was an enchanted city."

"A real city?" asks Shasta.

"Yes, honey, a real city."

"A city with deer?" asks Luke.

"Yes, honey, with deer." Columbia starts again. "Once upon a time there was an enchanted city next to the ocean whose citizens, favored by God, lived with great abundance, and were blessed with lights and bridges and spires and horses that never grew tired."

"Don't forget the deer," adds Luke.

"Yes, honey, and deer. And the citizens of the enchanted city were grateful for their blessings. But the enchanted city had only one problem, and the problem was that the sky above them would not bring forth rain.

"And so the enchanted city was bone dry—dry for so long its citizens could

Ed Dubrowsi/Archive Photos

barely remember the feel of water falling on their skins. Year after year the citizens of the city prayed for the rains, but year after year, the rains passed the city by. The prayers of the citizens continued—louder and louder—and *still* the rains would not arrive. The beauty and wonder of their city began to feel tainted, as though a curse had been placed upon them all.

"And then one day, a skeleton walked into the drought-stricken enchanted city, and the people of the city were afraid, thinking the skeleton must surely be connected to the drought.

"And the frightened king, standing before the skeleton, asked, 'Skeleton, who are you, and why have you visited our enchanted city?'

"And the skeleton said to the king, 'Who am I? I am *you*—I am the skeleton that lies inside you all. I have come to tell you to fear not—your city is not cursed as you think. But I have come instead to tell you a fact you all must know.'

"'What must we know, then?' asked the king, his legs clattering, as were those of his subjects.

"'You must know,' answered the skeleton, 'that while you pray for rain, you are also praying a different prayer—a prayer so deep and strong and insistent you are hardly able to know you are praying it.'

"'Oh, and what may this prayer be?' asked the king, now more curious than afraid.

"'It is simple,' replied the skeleton. 'While you live in mortal splendor—with glass elevators and silk shirts and grapes in December—the price you pay for your comfort is a collapsed vision of heaven—the loss of the ability to see pictures in your heads of an afterlife. You pray for rain, but you are also praying for pictures in your heads that will renew your faith in an afterlife.'"

Columbia gives a sideways glance; the children are drifting off.

"Well—the king and his citizens scoffed and, thinking the skeleton mad, lost their fears and sent him away from their city, and then once again they resumed their communal prayer for rain.

"But shortly after the skeleton's departure, the earth trembled, and the bridges shook and broke and the roads of the city tumbled down and the glass elevators cracked and the inexhaustible horses of the city were unable to ride and there was much destruction.

"The skeleton once again returned to the enchanted city and said to the king and the citizens who once again stood before him, 'I am the skeleton that lies within each and every one of you. I am the skeleton just underneath your lips, your eyeballs, your flesh—the skeleton that silently carries both your heart and your mind. And once more, I tell you that while you live in mortal splendor, the price you pay for this material comfort is a collapsed vision of heaven—an inability to see any longer pictures in your heads of an afterlife. You pray for rain, but you also, at a deeper level, pray for pictures in your heads that will renew your faith in an afterlife.'"

Luke asks if the citizens were grumpy people, but Columbia says no. They had tried hard to do their best, but they could only believe what they saw with their eyes. She says, "Well, once again the king and his citizens scoffed and they drove the skeleton from their city and resumed their prayers for rain, quickly forgetting the skeleton's words. And shortly thereafter a fire swept through the parched city and burned the houses of the rich and the houses of the good and the houses of the righteous. There was a great loss of beauty and the hearts of the city's people again were greatly hurt.

"And yet *again*, the skeleton came forth into the enchanted city and said to the citizens, 'Must I tell you a*gain*? You live in mortal splendor, yet the price you pay for this comfort is a collapsed vision of heaven—an inability to see any longer pictures in your head of an afterlife. You pray for rain, but you also pray for pictures in your heads that will renew your faith in an afterlife.'

"And yes, yet again the king and the citizens of the enchanted city cast the skeleton from its burned gates, continuing their prayers for rain and denying the skeleton's words. And shortly thereafter, another trial visited the city—the artists who would create and rebuild the burned-down houses and collapsed roads and bridges of the city began to sicken and die. The source of the city's beauty and wonder was being forever lost. And at this the king and the citizens wept furiously and said, 'Enough! Enough! We are losing our soul—something too valuable and irreplaceable is dying and we are powerless.'

"And so when the skeleton returned to the city one final time, the king said to him, 'O skeleton, we were wrong to have ignored your wise words. O skeleton, please—our suffering has become too great for us to bear. We are losing our soul. We realize now that our city's splendor tricked us into forgetting about death and the afterlife, and that we have secretly prayed for those images to appear to us to remind us of what lies beyond. But *please*, tell us what we need to know now to stop any further needless death and destruction from being visited upon ourselves.'

"And at *this*, the skeleton smiled his skeleton smile of teeth and calcium and bones and said, 'King, you have prayed for rain, but at a deeper level, you have also prayed for evidence to remind you, amid your splendor, of the death which does await us all. Accept the fact that as we live, we are also dead and all of your other prayers will be answered.'
    "'Thank you,' said the King. 'As I am alive, I am also dead.'

"And with this, the skeleton raised his bones to heaven and brought forth a bolt of lighting and a flood of rain onto the enchanted city—on its spires and bridges and roads and horses and glass elevators, and the citizens of the enchanted city fell to their knees in the rain amid their glittering abundance and thanked the skeleton for his generosity and then danced in honor of all that is good in this world and all that is good in the next."

Columbia looks at the sleeping children in the cool darkness of the van. These are her children; the grandchildren of her own hippie mother.
    Suddenly Columbia feels old, or rather, she feels she has reached the point

where she can never think of herself as being young again. She feels she has been a conduit through which has flowed an entity older and larger than herself—her mother, perhaps, or the ideas of her mother's times.

Years ago, Columbia once asked her mother, Melissa, what the sixties were like. Columbia greatly wanted to know how it *felt* to be alive then. Melissa, wistful, planting cilantro seeds in the soil-filled indentations of an egg carton, smiled, looked out the stained-glass window and said, "Honey, I'd love to tell you, but it was like a friend you loved very much who died of a horrible disease. While you might make new friends in your life, the new friends can never truly appreciate your old, dead friend because no matter how much you try to describe that dead friend, your new friends never knew the old friends when the old friends were alive. You just had to be there."

Despite the obliqueness of her reply, Melissa couldn't help but regale Columbia with endless tales of that long-gone era: tales of gardens and horses and moonlight and tear gas and beards and electricity. And from these tales, Columbia knows that at the heart of the sixties dream lies a core truth, a germ that refuses to die, an essence of purity and love that is open to abuse—and continually abused—but without which Columbia could not live her own life peacefully.

Columbia looks at the Coliseum. Any minute now Ezekiel will emerge, ready for the ride home. They will sleep in the parking lot tonight, she decides. In the *morning* they will drive home.

Anyhow, the concert is over. Columbia's face, feebly lit by Coliseum–parking lot sodium-vapor lights, is barely visible from outside the van's rain-beaded windows, and her face recedes into the depths of the vehicle, as though sinking into a deep dark pond. All that is visible now from outside the van is water dribbling down the roof onto its darkened glass. Water, water, ceaseless and nourishing, flowing everywhere—flowing down the Highway 24 tunnel up on the mountain, cascading from the Christmas lights garlanding nuclear aircraft carriers in the harbor, through the branches of eucalyptus trees that survived the fire—cold and clear, no hint of stopping—down all surfaces—over the oxidizing melted consumer durables in the Oakland Hills, into the dens of animals sleeping through the storm, through forgotten windows left open in the city—water, water, beating a drum on the roof of a van in a parking lot, the van in which Columbia's children are dreaming of a dancing skeleton. The skeleton that dances inside of me. The skeleton that dances inside of you.

Page 64: Ed Taylor/FPG; page 65: Gary Randall/FPG

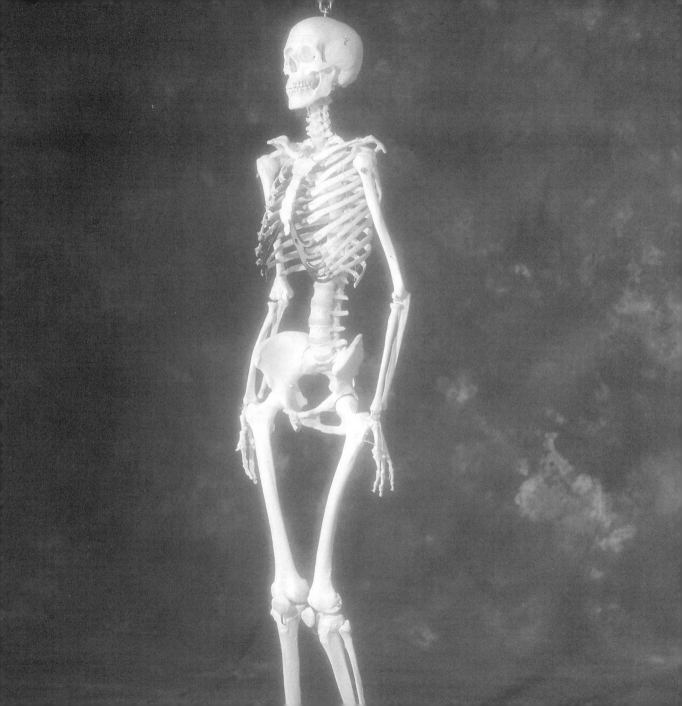

Part Two

Portraits of People and Places

11

LIONS GATE BRIDGE, VANCOUVER, B.C., CANADA

PERHAPS IN YOUR CITY THERE IS A STRUCTURE SO POTENT AND GLORIOUS THAT ITS existence in your mind becomes the actual *architecture* of your mind—a structure through which all of your dreams and ideas and hopes are funneled.

In my city, Vancouver, there is one such structure, a fairy-tale bridge called Lions Gate Bridge. Its three delicate spans link the city of Vancouver with the suburbs of the North Shore, where I grew up, and with the mountains and wilderness of British Columbia beyond those suburbs.

The only other road access to the North Shore is five miles down the harbor to the utilitarian and unfortunately rather charmless Second Narrows Bridge: a six-lane people-mover about which little more can be said without taxing the limits of charity.

Lions Gate Bridge is by no means a practical bridge—it looks to be spun from liquid sugar, and, unfortunately, it now seems to be dissolving like sugar. By urban planning and engineering standards it borders on being a disaster, but then isn't it true of life in general that nothing is more seductive than the dying starlet? The lost cowboy? The self-destructive jazz musician?

The bridge has three harrowingly narrow lanes. Depending on the time of day, commuters on the Lions Gate may have either one or two of these lanes apportioned to them. The rule of thumb is, tormentingly, the more traffic moving in your direction, the higher the probability of having only one lane.

But enough about the bridge's technicalities. We tolerate goodness knows how much from the people we love; the same goes for objects we love, too. I figure I have driven across the bridge maybe five or six thousand times in my life—that's all the way from Vancouver to Halifax and back—and never in all these miles have I once tired of the view, endlessly renewing, endlessly glorious.

Some of my happiest memories of Vancouver, or my life, for that matter, have been simple memories of driving across Lions Gate Bridge. In my mind, the AM radio is playing Heart's "Dreamboat Annie," the sulfur piles of North Vancouver shine their dim yellow hues, and the ocean and the boats and the mountains of West Vancouver shimmer like Tina Louise's gown.

Maybe I am headed to my parents' house or maybe I am off to the airport—the bridge's very existence is a metaphor for journey.

Like most regular Lions Gate Bridge drivers, I have my own little set of bridge quirks and observations. For example I get angry if I see a driver who discourteously breaks the one-two/one-two pattern of merging onto the north end: four lanes of traffic grudgingly, yet with decorum, braid into one.

Also, I have noticed that within moments of driving onto the bridge from the north end, most people instantly turn on their radios or stereos. I have no theory why they do this, but they just lunge for the dials.

As well, I have always noticed that traffic headed cityward mysteriously slows to a crawl once it hits the bridge's first draping span. It then shortly resumes its normal speed. I ascribe this predictable slowdown to people who are not from

Vancouver. When they suddenly encounter the beauty that surrounds them from mid-bridge—the quartz of the city to the south; the freighters below, plump with wheat and ore; the cruise liners tramping away off in the distance; as well as the swoop of the bridge above them—the out-of-towners are overwhelmed. They respond by jamming on their brakes.

In an odd way this makes me proud of my city—proud to live here. I never begrudge this inevitable slowdown.

For people who don't normally drive Lions Gate Bridge, discussion of bridge traffic by regular drivers can seem endlessly bothersome and incomprehensible:

"How was bridge traffic?"

"One lane."

"Standstill?"

"Yup."

"Both lanes the other way empty?"

"Yup."

"Ferry must have come in at Horseshoe Bay."

"I was going to take the Second Narrows but I thought Lions Gate would be clear after seven P.M."

"Do ferries arrive on the odd hour or the even hour?"

"Oh, and there was a stall . . ."

(*Insert scream from non-bridge driver here.*)

A bridge memory.

One night in 1982, shortly after midnight when art school had closed, I was driving in my old rusted yellow VW Rabbit through the Stanley Park causeway that funnels into the bridge toward the North Shore. Suddenly, the traffic in my lane ground to a stop and traffic in the lanes from the other direction vanished altogether.

Something was up.

I turned off my ignition and walked a short way nearer the bridge's south approach, where I quickly learned, as did the other drivers who emerged from their cars (with little question marks inside the thought balloons above their heads) that there was "a jumper" up in the bridge's riggings.

Ooohhh . . .

I headed back to my car to wait out the drama. Shortly, though, I began to hear horn music playing, live music, not a stereo, and I walked down to the mouth of the bridge, where a bearded man in a white suit stood on the roof of a white Cadillac parked between the two cement lions guarding the entrance. He was serenading the jumper on the bridge with "Stranger on the Shore."

The man with the horn was Frank Baker, a restaurant owner of that long-vanished era when "fine dining" meant a T-bone steak, three double scotches and a pack of Chesterfields.

Mr. Baker, who died in 1991, had once owned a "swinging" kind of restaurant in West Vancouver where your parents would take out-of-town guests, but only after first getting themselves all revved up with Herb Alpert records.

Mr. Baker was always, to younger eyes, the embodiment of a certain type of cool, so cool that he had even bought the original Aston Martin DB-5 used in the James Bond movie *Goldfinger.* He was certainly a character, and his restaurant was an occupational puppy mill for a good number of friends during high school who bussed there and diced the vegetables and did food-prep on weekends.

But Frank Baker was also a good musician, and that night on the bridge people like myself sat in the grass and daffodils along the banks of the causeway and listened to his songs, wondering, I guess, if we too might ever reach that point in life when we find ourselves in the riggings of Lions Gate Bridge, trying to decide *yes?* or *no?,* knowing that even if we decided *yes*, a water landing still offered a semblance of hope.

Another memory:

In late 1986 I arrived back in Vancouver after living abroad for a year. On that first evening back I looked down at the bridge and saw that it had been garlanded with brilliant pearls of light along its thin parabolic lines. I was shocked—it was so beautiful it made me lose my breath.

I asked my father about these lights, and he told me they were called "Gracie's Necklace," after a local politician. In the almost five decades since the bridge had been built, the city had been secretly dreaming of the day when it would cloak its bridge in light, and now the dream had become real life.

Now, whenever I fly back to Vancouver, it is Gracie's Necklace I look for from my seat, the sight I need to see in order to make myself feel I am home again. We often forget, living here in Vancouver, that we live in the youngest city on earth, a city almost entirely of, and *only* of, the twentieth century—and that this is Vancouver's greatest blessing. It is the delicacy of Gracie's Necklace that reminds me we live, not so much in a city but in a dream of a city.

Now, I was not a particularly standout student in high school. I seem to remember spending the bulk of those years more or less catatonic from understimulation. One of the few respites from the school's daily underdosings of learning was the view from up the mountain of the bridge, the city, Mount Baker, of Vancouver Island and of the never-ending cranes continually transforming the skyline.

In October, the fogs would roll in; the city below became a glowing, foaming prairie of white light. Lions Gate Bridge would puncture through that light, glowing gold, offering transport into that other, luminous arena.

For grades 8, 9, 10 and most of grade 11, I spent many hours slumped over the physics class radiator, dreaming of the day—January 13, 1978—two weeks after my sixteenth birthday, when I would pass my driver's test and at last be able to drive into that magic city bathed in light.

Curiously, I had my sixteenth birthday dinner at Frank Baker's restaurant— now almost *exactly* half-a-lifetime ago. Birthday gift: Solomon 555 ski bindings and a down vest. The food: Frank Baker's buffet table—all the warm Jell-O you could eat. Michelle, Caroline and Michael—do they remember as I do that silly, forgettable evening, back so long ago when we were all still young?

*   *   *

Recently there has been talk of tearing down Lions Gate Bridge, and such talk truly horrifies me. People speak of Lions Gate Bridge as being merely a tool, a piece of infrastructure that can be casually deleted, plundered from our memories with not a second thought to the consequences its vanishing might have on our interior lives.

I think that when people begin to talk like this, they are running scared—they are doing something that I know I do myself: I try to disguise what I am really feeling by saying and doing the opposite thing. The bridge is *not* merely a tool, not a casually deletable piece of infrastructure, and it can never be deleted from memories like an undesirable file.

I can't do this with Lions Gate Bridge anymore. Why was it so hard until recently for me to simply say that the bridge is a thing of delicate beauty—an intricate part of my life and memories? Why is it so hard for all of us to say loudly and clearly to each other that the bridge is an embodiment of grace and charm and we must not let it die?

Why would we destroy something we love rather than let a stupid pride prevent us from saying, "It means something to me"?

I never said what happened the night of the jumper.

After an hour or so, the jumper came down and was promptly whisked away by a screaming ambulance. Frank Baker came down off the roof of his Cadillac, took his bows to our claps, and he drove away.

I myself got back into my old Rabbit and drove across the bridge, but the bridge felt different that night, as though it led me to a newer, different place.

I want you to imagine you are driving north, across the Lions Gate Bridge, and the sky is steely gray and the sugar-dusted mountains loom blackly in the distance. Imagine what lies behind those mountains—realize that there are only *more* mountains—mountains until the North Pole, mountains until the end of the world, mountains taller than a thousand me's, mountains taller than a thousand you's.

Here is where civilization ends; here is where time ends and where eternity begins. Here is what Lions Gate Bridge is: one last grand gesture of beauty, of charm, and of grace before we enter the hinterlands, before the air becomes too brittle and too cold to breathe, before we enter that place where life becomes harsh, where we must become animals in order to survive.

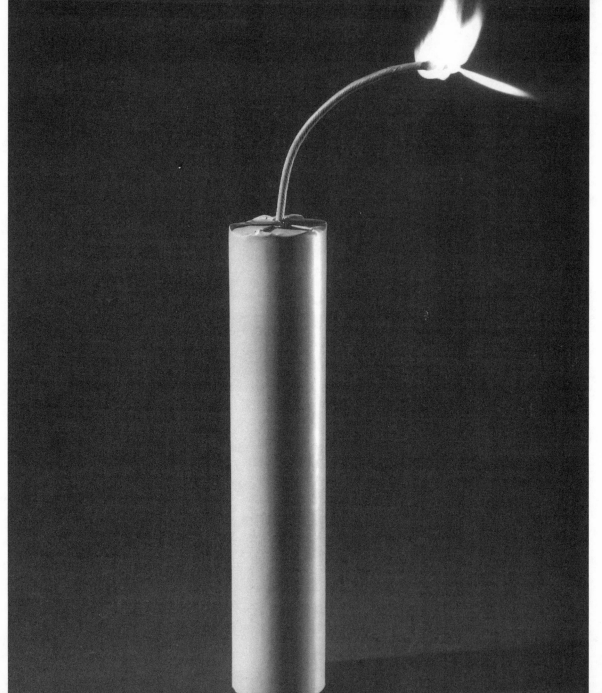

12

THE GERMAN REPORTER

May 27, 1994

A REPORTER FROM A GERMAN MAGAZINE WAS SCHEDULED TO ARRIVE, AND I WAS dreading it.

In the previous two weeks I had visited, on separate trips, San Francisco, Copenhagen, Austin and Washington, D.C. My sense of internal time had snapped from jet lag.

Too many hotels and airports had also left me geographically dislocated—feeling as though I was from nowhere. As well, I had been working too hard of late. My ability to be polite to strangers had diminished. I was expecting nothing from this encounter with the German reporter.

The reporter had been flying for thirty-seven hours when he got to Vancouver (via LAX via Frankfurt from Hamburg). His own sense of time and place had pretty much snapped, and because of this, I was prepared to be more sympathetic toward him than I might be normally to a reporter.

When we finally met in the Hyatt lobby, I was struck by how much he reminded me of myself when I was twenty-four nearly a decade before. Despite his jet lag, he was obviously a good-natured sort—enthusiastically lost, asking too many questions, unfamiliar with hotel voice-mail systems and wearing clothes that will look charmingly dated in photos ten years from now. He had a "soul patch" on his chin and a DEG (Düsseldorf Eis Gemeinschaft) baseball cap worn backward. And this was pretty much *me* at twenty-four.

I have always seen twenty-four as a charmed year. It was the year I lost my sense of being young—but that's another story. It's reassuring to see people deal with being twenty-four better than the way we dealt with it, which is never too well.

Anyway, it was a Pacific blue sky Thursday. We ate a quick curry rice at a Japanese noodle dive on Robson Street, and I decided, somewhat rashly, that the German reporter was some form of Dickens-like ghost of myself past, come to visit me in my current state of tiredness for reasons unknown.

As such, I felt obligated to show this spirit my world, something I normally never do. I thought this German reporter might be able to help me fix my damaged sense of damaged time and space. If I could help him deal with being twenty-four, fine, but I didn't tell him this.

Oh—the things we should have known when we were younger. . . .

We drove to the North Shore and hiked through Capilano Canyon, through the Douglas firs and yellow cedars and hemlocks—the canyon in the mountain just below the subdivision where I grew up. The sun shone brightly through the lower canopy of leaves—maples, mainly—and inside the taller trees it was cool and dark and quiet and the light was green.

We saw a woodpecker. The bird's head glistened red like undried blood, and it was pecking a hole in a dead hemlock tree. We sat on the twisting path quietly, and we sat for long enough that our hearts slowed down their beating, and we watched the woodpecker, not a spit away, and it seemed to not care that we existed.

In the river below, there were steelhead minnows and fishermen looking for bigger fish. And down this canyon flew a kingfisher with a blue-and-white crested head, cruising the canyon's twists like a Toyota purring down a California freeway.

We ate cherries and spat the pits into the river.

We visited the salmon hatchery—the incubator in which coho, chum and sockeye salmon spawn and in which they die and in which they are born.

I told the German reporter that in literature, birds are ideas and fish are souls, and that metaphor surrounds us—and that all you need to do is be still and to ask, and the right metaphor will always present itself to you.

After the canyon we drove the two miles up Capilano Road to Grouse Mountain, where I spent many of my teenage years skiing. We rode the tramway to the top; our gondola was full of forty-three senior citizens. These were the "Rambling Rovers" of Coeur d'Alene, Idaho: forty-three teensy little people like Franklin Mint figurines with white hair, all wearing blue rayon baseball jackets. These old people were, in fact, all *so* identical that it spooked us. The German reporter and I wondered if that was our fate, no matter how hard we tried, to become a Rambling Rover roaming the world in pursuit of meaning from within an Evergreen Coachline bus with Oregon license plates.

Up at the top of the mountain, we rode a helicopter and roamed the alps behind the city of Vancouver. In this helicopter, up in those heights, we saw melting reservoirs, virgin forests and islands in the Pacific like lead coins in an ocean of gold. And we saw the glaciers and the wild rivers that stretch until the end of the world.

Afterward in a James Bond–like restaurant on top of the mountain, we discussed civilization and we looked down on the cloudless, flawless suburb of my youth below. I told the German reporter that he had seen today something I had always suspected but had only recently articulated: that as humans we are always on the brink of wilderness—that we are always animals first—that civilization is an act of political will, and not a given right. And that middle-class peace is something to be cherished, not mocked, because without it, we are lost, and we are only animals and never anything more.

By the time we returned to the tramway, the senior citizens had vanished. Instead there was a local high school field trip and kids yelling "Sean!" and "Kelly!" and "Heather!" and "Jamie!" at each other, and I had this feeling—as though the Rambling Rovers had come to the mountain, received the word of God, and been given a second chance at youth. I felt as though something was beginning to be reborn.

After the mountain we visited a cheeseburger hangout where a girl I once knew, an old friend, used to work. I hadn't seen her in many years and I asked the manager if he had seen her lately. He said yes—just a month before, it turned out. And so I asked if she was happy and he said, as diplomatically as he could, *not really*.

I was sad, because we want the people we care about, even if they have vanished from our day-to-day lives, to find some measure of happiness. I was sad because unhappiness is something we are never taught about; we are taught to expect happiness, but never a Plan B to use in its absence.

May 28, 1994

The next day was sunny too, and I picked up the German reporter, and we did some of my daily stuff—mailed letters, visited FedEx—and we had coffee at a pretentious coffee bar where all the people try to look like MTV stars and fashion models.

The German reporter asked me what it means to be "real," which is, when you think about it, an extraordinary question. Each of these people in the coffee bar, sneaking peeks at themselves reflected in the framed artwork, considered themselves to be more "real" than the other people sneaking the same peeks. What, exactly, does *real* mean? Are you real? Am I real? Was this German reporter real? How real *is* real?

The German reporter and I then drove through Kitsilano along Point Grey to Spanish Banks, where the tide was *way* out. We walked in the muddy sand and his shoes—these ridiculous billiard green "French Foreign Legion" shoes—got soaked, and so he removed them. We looked at the holes in the wet sand made by the breathing clams, and it seemed to us as though the planet was breathing.

Some people near us, tourists probably, were mystified that the tide could be so low—that a person could almost walk across the sea to the mountains on the other side.

One of the men in the group said, "Hey—let's walk across the water to that ship out there." The phrase stuck in my mind because he was, I think, made temporarily dizzy by the thought that this might actually be possible.

We then drove out to the Nitobe Japanese Gardens at the University of British Columbia, and I took my shoes off too, and we walked through the Japanese garden. Although it is a manufactured version of wilderness, like a seventeenth-century Disneyland, it is still beautiful.

Our feet walked over the pebbles and the cool moss and the smooth stones and the zigzag bridge over the blooming irises. The Japanese build bridges in zigzags because after you walk across them, evil spirits get confused and fall off the edges. We felt them fall.

Then we got back in the car and went to shop for used tapes and records and CDs at a store in Kitsilano. I quickly found what *I* wanted: *Alice Cooper's Greatest Hits* and *Koyaanisqatsi* by Philip Glass, and I sat on a step while the German reporter prowled around. I made notes in my notebook—casual voices and things we had heard and seen over the past day that made more sense than other things, and this is what I wrote in my book:

- *I was walking down the street and suddenly I felt I had lost something, but I didn't know what.* (The German reporter had said this as we were leaving the car earlier.)
- *I was young and not a soul had found my soul.* (A song that was playing on the store's stereo.)
- *Please wait patiently during the silence.* (A recorded voice spoken to me by a Toronto Dominion Bank answering machine that morning.)
- *I could happily die right now with nothing but today in my eyes.* (A line written by Truman Capote I had read in a book the night before.)

For dinner we visited Cameron and Wendy, two of my best friends in the world, at their house in Shaughnessy. We ordered pizza and sat in the kitchen until it got dark. We lit candles and around eleven, their four-month-old daughter, Rachael, cried, and Wendy brought her down to the kitchen. Rachael, my goddaughter, glowed in the candles, so obviously created out of love by my two friends that it made me speechless to know that such pure love can, and does, exist, and when such a feeling is encountered, no words need to be spoken, so for a short while there was a pure silence.

May 29, 1994

The next day it rained and I was happy, because this is how Vancouver usually is and how it feels. The German reporter and I took a ferry to a small island called Bowen Island for lunch. Afterward we returned to the mainland and drove up the fjord of Howe Sound, up Highway 99.

We drove to Britannia Beach, a tiny town next to a river that floods every three years, although its people never move. They just patch up their houses and stay. People are odd.

We parked the car and walked down the Pacific Great Western train tracks a

half-mile to an old herring boat beached like a whale back in the 1940s, majestic and sad. I told the German reporter that this boat was a symbol for a dignified, magnificent death.

And I remembered two days previously, when the two of us were in the forest, running our hands through the soil in the roots of a fir tree, feeling the soil's dry coolness sifting through our fingers, deciding that I would rather be buried than cremated, because you give more back to the earth that way.

Not in a casket. But just buried.

In a forest.

We walked back through the rainforest to the train tracks. Farther down the tracks there was a tunnel, and I told him my theory that we instinctively wave to people on trains because trains are a metaphor for being alive: countless souls, trapped together, hurtling across the landscape, with a destination somewhere in the unseeable distance.

Nobody ever waves at buses.

I told him how once, in a Metroliner train passing through Delaware, I waved from the train to some people going under the train bridge on a speedboat. It had the feel of a one-night stand with somebody you know you might have fallen in love with had there been enough time.

We walked through the tunnel, and inside, in its middle, all we could hear was the sound of the German reporter's Aiwa tape recorder running, so he turned it off. And then we heard nothing.

We walked out the tunnel, into the light on the other side, and I said that dying was maybe like this: When we looked back at the tunnel, the curve made it look much shorter going back than it did the other way.

On the way back at the side of the track we found a stick of dynamite, a red M-2000 used by the railway companies for blasting granite. It looked like cartoon dynamite, like from an *Itchy and Scratchy* cartoon. We were going to pick up the stick, but then I realized the nitroglycerine inside might explode. So we did a totally stupid thing and threw big rocks at it to try to make it blow up. Nothing happened—and because dynamite isn't really the sort of thing one is allowed to pack in one's luggage on transatlantic flights, we decided to just leave it alone and not take it as a souvenir.

But if we ever need a stick of dynamite, we know where to find one. This is not a bad thing to know.

And then we both got really dozy, and we drove into a small redneck town called Squamish and sat in a coffee shop and watched pickup trucks cruise by. After an hour we drove back into Vancouver and stopped at my apartment for me to pick up my messages and to change clothes. For a souvenir I gave the German reporter an old white T-shirt that I asked him to put on. Then, with a thick Sharpie permanent black felt-tip marker I wrote on it the corrected wording of the Truman Capote quote I had written incorrectly earlier in my note pad. I wrote:

> As for me
> I could leave the world
> with today
> in my eyes.
> —t.c.

We had a late dinner with my friend James, one of the smartest people I know. We discussed the notion of "being real" with him—and of being "hyper-real" and "post-human" and I don't think we arrived at any definite answer, but it's important to know people who think about these things.

At 11:30 P.M. I dropped the German reporter off at the Hyatt. He had to be awake at 4:30 A.M. to go to the airport. He was gracious and thanked me for my time over the past few days, but instead I thanked *him*.

*   *   *

Days.

We lose our days—and our ability to retrieve them—and yet there are some days that should never be lost.

I left the German reporter, this younger ghost of myself, probably forever, on the Hyatt doorstep. My sense of time felt, if not healed, then reconciled. I don't know about his.

It was prom night in Vancouver, and the hotel's front area was a sea of limousines and high school graduates: children—babies, really—dressed in their finest ball gowns and tuxedos, all of them flush with the knowledge that tonight was supposed to be the best night of their life, that tonight was the night they would take with them to the grave.

The German reporter and I were invisible to these teenagers because we did not belong in their universe of extreme youth. And I remembered my own prom night—my Peter Frampton hairdo, my light-blue tuxedo and the cars that would also take me off into the night.

Oh, how I *wish* those children could read those words I felt-penned on the German reporter's chest—those words that forever lie behind Superman's written "S"—those words I had written in a permanent ink that soaked through the T-shirt's old cotton fabric and through his foreign skin and into his bloodstream—and, I would hope, into the heart of this ghost of my earlier self.

13

POSTCARD FROM
THE FORMER EAST BERLIN

(CIRCUS ENVY)

BERLIN, MONDAY, OCTOBER 3, 1994, FIVE YEARS AFTER THE WALL THING HAPPENED. Shopping is a joke; consumption has not nourished. Five years later the market-place is a bore. And the Walled landscape—once overwhelmingly tragic and melancholic—is now overwhelmingly ironic and frantic and just plain sad. But then does this come as news?

A free Elton John concert is scheduled for the Brandenburg Gate on October 3. The Gypsy Kings, Paul Young and the Leningrad Cowboys will also be there. Karl Marx Allee is peppered with posters for Barry Manilow and liberal SDP candidate Rudolf Scharping.

Wordless Helmut Kohl posters feature a beaming Kohl as Santa-Claus-minus-the-beard flanked by smiling young people. A local artist has placed UNITED COLORS OF BENNETON stickers atop the Kohl posters, and there is no sense of incongruity or any seeming alteration of meaning.

*　　*　　*

The Saturday afternoon before October 3, I was at a MusicCity in the Alexanderplatz, a former ideological showplace where isotopes of Socialist Modernism compete for Miss Uncongeniality, where plaza sculptures of almost-indescribable dreariness make one ache for the whimsical frivolity of a Richard Serra or a Donald Judd. I asked a salesclerk politely enough, *"Hello, do you have the new R.E.M. album?"* and was rebuffed with a bored, contemptuous, *"Nein."*

Okayyyyyy.

Meanwhile, sitting beside this clerk stood a stack of the same aforementioned R.E.M. album, *Monster*. So I said to the gentleman, *"Hmmm, well, in that case, I'll have one of* those *instead."*

With a gesture blending loathing, ennui, disgust and patronization, the album was hurled onto the counter, the clerk then bracing his arms across his chest in a listless, disengaged challenge.

I handed over my VISA card, only to be rewarded with a withering, *"VISA? . . . Nein."*

Cash was proffered and the *Monster* album and the mingiest of plastic bags thrown into my face. Back in the ex-DDR, the retail concept is still, five years later, something that might need just the smallest splash of Total Quality Management.

When I mention this incident to West Berlin friends, they roll their eyes and say *"DDR."* As an adjective describing service, "DDR" combines *Fawlty Towers* with Stalinism.

A mile west, at the corner of Unter den Linden begins the Friedrichstrasse recon-struction—a dead showcase neighborhood transformed once again into a newer showcase neighborhood for a new regime: six square blocks made over with untold billions of Deutsch marks. Signs EIN LUXURY HOTEL; French superstar architect Jean Nouvel has designed a new Galeries Lafayette, nearly completed and hemmed at the bottom with strips of marigold, navy and aubergine.

In a continent that seems at best hesitant to generate new skylines, the thin chopstick-like forms of the construction cranes over Friedrichstrasse become what skyline there will be in this decade, at least. It is a post-national architecturescape that contrasts vividly with what filled the neighborhood before. The streets are rife with the lawnmower rumbles of Trabants and Wartburgs that compete with the thrums of South Beach aqua-colored Toyota Supras.

In this epicenter of irony, Havana-caliber consumer time-technology collisions occur every three feet. Along nearby Unter den Linden, ex-Stasi members driving Korean-built taxis gaze longingly at the ex-Stasi disco, which is now a T.G.I. Fridays and a Radisson Hotel Plaza. One can only imagine earnest midwestern Radisson executives refitting the hotel and discovering cobwebbed Soviet Beta recording cameras behind cobwebbed bedroom mirrors. The nearby Palast der Republik, resembling a failed entry for an LBJ Library design competition and where Erich Honnecker pursued his private realms, is quarantined because of asbestos poisoning and is locally named *"der Asbesthaus."*

Friedrichstrasse's newly constructed landscape is one of infrastructural pornography. Aboveground water pipes punctuate the landscape like the Mad Mouse at the local Fun World; pools of silicon resin drip into the sandy Prussian soil like a thousand breast implants fallen off the back of a truck.

An Apple computer training school overlooks workers in orange and blue overalls who weld I-beams while Saran-Wrap'ing dead socialist architecture in green net veils like the scarves around Grace Kelly's neck. Furukawa backhoes excavate piles of soil of varying historical molarity. There are stacks of gas cylinders and cable spools; on Französischestrasse, black telecom cables coil beneath one's feet as they descend into the earth. Stacks of Crisco-smooth Kalksandstein bricks, like Joseph Beuys sculptures, rest beside hexagon-shaped dumpsters filled with dead rusty rebar and sandy, asbestos-choked Eastern bloc cement. Modular preassembled window components are lifted into the air by cranes with names like Liebherr. Fresh black pavement is stained with splashes of lime. There are Dixi portable toilets and random sewage odors. Jackhammers drill away at statist architecture; polyurethane foam extrudes from underneath wood planks above the U-Bahn.

*   *   *

Back at the hotel, like any good pop-music enthusiast, I listened to my new album several dozen times while reading the wrapper notes, in this case a special 48-page mini-book. My favorite song on the tape is one called "Circus Envy," a roaring, secret-agent-feeling number describing jealousy—a monster whose symbol is a headless bear that appears on the mini-book's cover. The title song contains the line, "*Here comes that awful feeling again*," which resonates for me the rest of my stay, reinforced by the image of the bear cub, which is the civic emblem of the city of Berlin.

The citizens of former East Berlin have had to make the leap from 1945 to 1995. They never had a 1960s, '70s, '80s or even a '90s. They want what the West has, and they think that they are slowly, grudgingly and surely joining the West every day. Acid-wash denim clothing is seen as a symbol of shooting too far too quickly and has been banished from the landscape, due, no doubt, for a revival in ten minutes or so.

But there is no language in the East to make sense of Friedrichstrasse's Deutsche Interhotel GmbH, minibars, non-smoking attitudes, baby vegetables or movie-studio-style politics. The people of the East think they are entering the West, but they are actually entering the era of the transnational. It is a mistake to confuse the amoral forces of transnationalism with the West. The instantaneous transfer of capital from one node to another is not what the West was ever about.

The Ossis, the ex-Easterners, greet you, a Wessi, almost invariably with "Hello, *I'm confused.*" The Ossis recognize their own crisis, but explain to them that the West is in crisis as well—a crisis more sublime because the West has already seen a world of desire based purely on consumption—and they know the hollowness lying at its core.

Ossis want what the Wessis have—that's obvious. But try and tell Ossis that what they now think they desire is something pointless, and they will accuse you of trying to deny them the plunder of consumption sheerly out of spite. Try to tell people that they can't have what they think they really want—that just won't work.

A big political question currently facing Germany, if not the entire West, is, What is it we can now desire now that things, objects—*stuff*—has failed us? The engineering of sustaining, nourishing new models of desire: that is the new issue. Even the East Germans express fear about the Chinese manufacturing a people's car—a current event that like no other pinpoints the unsustainability of the dream of consumption.

Does the ghost of post-WWII-reconstructionist Konrad Adenauer walk amid this Friedrichstrasse landscape—a landscape more reminiscent of Orange County than that of Frederick the Great? Has the emblematic bear cub of Berlin turned into the bear of the California Republic?

No, Konrad Adenauer would not walk here. A spectating ghost would have to be the ghost of somebody transnational, somebody as yet undefined—a Beast whose aesthetic is one of absolute function and absolute function only. A creature of Facadism, of instantaneous transglobal currency transfers—a creature who is hostile to culture and who gives us entry into the realms of surrealism without providing any underlying subconscious. A headless bear of jealousy that slouches through the Brandenburg Gate, not knowing what it wants, only that it wants more.

Here comes that awful feeling again.

14

LETTER TO KURT COBAIN

[WHAT'S ON YOUR POWERBOOK? THE FOLLOWING PIECE, MINUS THE LAST TWO paragraphs, was written in early March 1994, when Kurt Cobain entered the American Hospital in Rome. The small final addendum was added in April upon news of the discovery of his body at his home in Bellevue, Washington.]

Friday, April 8, 1994

Dear Kurt,

I was in Seattle, March 4, 1994, when I heard the news—that you were in Rome—that you drank too much champagne, took too many sedatives, Rohypnol—had the flu. Whatever. You were in a coma. I once lived in Italy in 1984, and I remember that the pharmacists

Ed Sirrs/Retna Pictures

there dispense downers like they were Pez. So the news sounded believable.

Representatives of David Geffen's record company kept giving out the same story over the wires—semi-news: *Kurt has opened his eyes—Kurt squeezed his hand in response to his name.* But nobody in Seattle felt as if they knew any real news. One is either in a coma or one is *not* in a coma.

Apocrypha and half-truths breezed through the city. In the end it was always the same: *No, Kurt's still in a coma . . . we think.* Reuters admitted that previous reports of your being out of the coma were incorrect.

Everyone's reflexive response was to make a joke about it all, but in the end we couldn't. Inside us there are 33⅓ records, and to make a joke about you would have been to scratch a needle across that record; irony was jettisoned. We made jokes instead about record companies and about Italian ambulances and about hospital food, but never about *you.* The radio station played your songs over and over, always with the same news story—*no news.*

Around 3:00 I had to drive from downtown along Interstate-5 to Kent, past the KingDome, where I once went to see Paul McCartney and Wings back in the 1970s. And just then the radio played your song, "Dumb," and I saw a clump of cherry trees that had been tricked by an early spring into blooming, and I started to cry.

It had been raining in Seattle for weeks.

The day you went into your coma was the first day the sky had even considered clearing up. It was one of those can't-make-up-its-mind days. Storm clouds brooded over Elliot Bay and Lake Washington, yet it was also sunny—or kind of sunny—over the Boeing fields and south toward Tacoma. The sky over Seattle became the city's heart that day—it felt as though the sky were trying to decide whether to shine or whether to forget.

In Kent, I drove past a hotel project that had failed, and its tar-papered walls had unraveled like mummy's cloth and were flapping in the wind, like a hotel covered in bandages; it had no windows. In the middle of a plowed field I saw a rhododendron in bloom. Pink.

The radio still had no news. Along Interstate 5 the arbutus trees rustled in the wind, and the undersides of their leaves—the sides that gather oxygen—were flashing sage-colored against the freeway's embankment. And I remembered being younger and visiting Seattle from Vancouver—my most compelling memory of that city was of a half-completed freeway that led off into nowhere.

And I kept thinking of some of the fields I had just seen, now barely turning to green, and how these fields reminded me of fears I had when I was younger—fears that nature might simply decide not to wake up one year. Nature would open her eyes, go back to sleep, and never return.

I drove up to the University District where the students were in a sort of fog. The guy at the counter at the record shop didn't know anything. I began seeing only symbols that fit the situation: I saw a young woman standing on a corner in a floral dress and army boots taking Polaroids of nothing; on Denny Way I saw a bike courier pulling an empty bike alongside him; back at the hotel I lost a pair of nine-dollar sunglasses through a hole in my pocket—glasses I had always liked because they made the sky seem bluer than it really is.

On KIRO-TV, on the 6:30 news broadcast they showed *the ambulance* taking you away to the American Hospital.

Italy.

You, this child of *here*, of newness, lost in the oldest of cities. It seemed cruel.

Later that night there was *still* no real news. But at least it seemed as though you were out of your coma. But then a *new* dread emerged, one so bad that we couldn't even talk about it directly, as though the words would give the dread life of its own—the dread that you might emerge from your coma . . . brain dead. So instead my friends and I talked about the weather. We tried to establish if, in fact, the sky that day had been sunny or rainy. It was such a close call that nobody could say for sure. Night had fallen before it could be made conclusive, before we could be totally sure that the sun had won.

You were apparently fine the next day. At the hospital you asked for a strawberry milkshake when you woke up. You were not brain dead. Or so it seemed. And the world went on.

But I also remember noting that I never saw a picture of you after that day—not even a shot of you leaving Europe, leaving the past—or a shot of you flashing the peace sign for the press. And then yesterday I heard Nirvana had pulled out of the Lollapalooza Tour. And I figured *some*thing was up.

And now you are dead.

I was in San Francisco, driving up the 101 past Candlestick Park when the news came over the radio, LIVE 105—the news that you had shot yourself.

A few minutes later I was in the city and I pulled the car over and tried to figure out what I felt.

I had never asked you to make me care about you, but it happened—against the hype, against the odds—and now you are in my imagination forever.

And I figure you're in heaven, too. But how, exactly does it help you *now*, to know that you, too, as it is said, were once adored?

D.

15

HAROLDING IN
WEST VANCOUVER

IN BRITAIN THERE IS A SUBGROUP OF CITIZENS CALLED TRAIN-SPOTTERS WHO SPEND their afternoons sitting on railway embankments clocking the passage of local trains. In North America there is a certain subgroup of teens—"Harolds"—obsessed with hanging about cemeteries, continually witnessing the passage of life into death. (Etymology: the seventies cult-film classic *Harold and Maude*, in which a young man obsessed with death frequents funerals and graveyards as a hobby.)

I was once very much a Harold.

The cemetery I frequented was the Capilano View Cemetery, the municipal burial ground of West Vancouver, located in the British Properties—a hillside Pacific Palisades/Glendale-ish suburb of Vancouver that was spawned, *ex nihilo*, from the West Coast rain forests mid-century. (Its growth continued well into the seventies.)

From about the ages of eighteen to twenty-one, I Harolded away almost weekly at the Capilano View Cemetery, sitting on its benches, strolling among its neatly mown stones, seeing who had died when, and at what age. Implicit in the act of being a Harold is hubris, a self-conscious notion of one's own immortality. Harold laughs in the face of death (*har har!*), and, most important, he derives a specific hit of pleasure from knowing death exists, yet not fearing it.

Capilano View Cemetery is the only part of the British Properties to have any history of credible duration. Its first burial was in February 1926. The cemetery's topiaried ilexes, yews, cedars, spruces and cherries, are all aged roughly fiftysomething, and thus supply the suburb's young Harolds (I was not alone) with visible, capital-H history simply not available locally at the Park Royal Shopping Centre (1950) or amid the post-and-beam Homes of Tomorrow flanked by split-leaf Japanese maples lining the British Properties' steep, twisting streets.

Capilano View's ten spartan acres speak of Mies Van der Rohe's uncompromising minimalism; no protrusive tombstones are allowed (all stones are flush with the soil and ideal for Friday-night Frisbee throws); all "floral offerings" must fit into cups recessed into the soil so that the container does not peek above the earth's surface. Plastic flowers are allowed only between November 1 and April 1. The cemetery is flanked, to the north and east, by a great West Coast rain forest. There are rhododendrons; there are monkey-puzzle trees.

Harold Lit: I used to read stories about tea planters and rubber-plantation owners who died in hot climates and were buried on the same day, for fear of rot, in lands far away from home. Part of growing up in West Vancouver was to feel as if you were growing up in the middle of nowhere: a zero-history, zero-ideology bond-issuing construct teetering on the edge of the continent. Oh, how I identified with those tea planters! To be buried on the edge of nowhere is to question one's sense of existence. Who *are* we, if we have no landscape to call our own?

I often visit cemeteries whenever I am in a new city: They are often a city's locale of greatest respite. Toronto's Mount Pleasant is as silent as the womb; Tokyo's Akasaka cemetery is usually nearly empty save for a few specialized visiting days and has the sloppy, stacks-of-dishes feel of a bachelor's apartment.

Cemetery architecture tells us much about the way a culture relates to its ancestry. Mexico's dazzling, almost optically painful marzipan crypt confections convey a they-are-still-alive rapport with the departed; Ireland's mournful, lichen-encrusted Celtic crosses, snaggletoothed over tufts of unscythed bracken, speak of loneliness—and of the acceptance that we all live with one foot in the grave. And West Vancouver's highly municipally ordinated, gridded and near-invisible gravestones treat dying as a low-fuss return to the nature that is contained in the rain forest enclosing the graveyard. One's soul is simply ATM'ed into the forest next door.

I stopped being a Harold because of one particular incident: In the summer of 1983 I was playing a toy xylophone on a cement bench at the extreme east edge of the cemetery. I was trying to duplicate the opening sequence of notes from Orchestral Manoeuvres in the Dark's 1981 hit, "Joan of Arc" (a brief flirtation with Catholicism).

A few days later, reading a copy of the local biweekly *North Shore News* at a local Midas Muffler shop, I learned that there had been a grave robbery at the cemetery not a day after I had been playing the xylophone—and not far from my prized Harold's bench. A decayed head, or other body parts had been exhumed and stolen, thieves unknown.

Well, that was *that*—I immediately ceased Harolding the Capilano View. Mortality (in the form of the most depressing ilk of trailer-park evil) had crept in from the forest and invaded my pristine Harolding site. I remember being depressed and terrified at somehow being implicated in this random and seamy debauch. And to clinch my avoidance of the cemetery, the newspapers also soon gave the news that West Vancouver was about to chainsaw and expand a further five acres of rain forest adjoining the cemetery's lovely north side.

Expansion in the New World is invariably at the expense of nature—never at the expense of previously existing structures. And to someone completely of the New World, the ravaging can be too painful to watch.

Ciao, Harold.

I returned to Capilano View recently, though—ten years later. By one's early thirties, loss in all of its forms invariably makes its presence known. I felt an urgent need to visit Harold's old stomping grounds.

It was not a sunny day as I revisited Capilano View, and I was surprised by what I saw. Yes, its Miesian green fields, flat as billiard tables, were unchanged. But the five-acre chainsawed clear-cut to the north had been left to go to seed. I had been expecting a brand-new golf green peppered with grave markers; instead the ex-forest sprouted a dense, furry hippie's beard of several thousand leafless alder trees—millions of ganglions of leafless branches, poking upward, all of them receding into the fog upon the hill, like brain dendrites cultured on a sterile agar, no longer connected to a sentient being and hence incapable of thought.

Mixed feelings: the fact that the forest had not been destroyed—merely "repurposed" as an alder glade—might, at first, seem like a reprieve, but it was not. An alder is a weed tree, which, by B.C. standards, is a mere precursor of destruction that has not yet been fully completed—destruction on hiatus. Alders mean that the bulldozers have yet to arrive; alders mean that the Circle K mini-mart is still being designed; alders mean that the complete erasure of Nature is still yet to come. A field of Kentucky bluegrass would have at least betokened some form of completion; alders instead betokened Nature having her back broken on the rack.

But this is tree-hugger talk.

"It's a B.C. thing."

Whatever.

The fact is that I felt oh-so-much older standing next to this brain-dead glade, this copse of erased memory. Its millions of thick, chewy wet branches, three times my own height, all bunched ridiculously close together, comprised a challenge to me—a challenge impossible to refuse.

And so, forgetting propriety, and soaking my sweater and pants and shoes, I stepped into this monoculture of wet cellulose fronds—into its mud and into its leather-strap branches that slapped my face, trudging deeper and deeper, as though into a field of tall, tall corn—and I went out looking for Harold.

16

TWO POSTCARDS FROM THE BAHAMAS

POSTCARD ONE:
THE WHOLE WORLD
AND AN ENTIRE LIFE
IN A DAY

I WALK AROUND THE ISLAND AND I SEE MOMENTS OF BEAUTY THAT DAZZLE ME WITH their transience: sunset inside a wall built of green bottles up above the graveyard; a hibiscus flower inside a bottle atop the wall; a yellow moth atop a yellow flower. These small moments become memories.

I think I am losing my memory, and while I know it's natural, I think I'm too young for this to be starting, and it frightens me a bit. I was thinking about this early this morning while I was walking down an Island road.

There was a hurricane here a few years ago and many trees fell down and many houses lost their roofs. Roads that once had shade now sit in blinding sun, and once-familiar landscapes now confuse.

As well as being worried about losing my memory, another thing is happening, which doesn't frighten me, but *does* concern me: I am starting to confuse my dream life with my waking life.

"Didn't I already take that medicine?"

"But I *did* return that library book."

"I once walked down this road before, but wasn't it different then?"

This morning I figured that if you lose your memory more or less completely, then each individual day becomes your entire life—because the next day you've already forgotten what came before. For a person with no memory, existence becomes a chain of discrete, day-to-day lives.

So anyway, today I figured that since this is where I'm headed anyway, I might as well attempt to see today itself as representative of my whole life, or rather, as a whole life unto itself.

I didn't do a great deal today, but simply by being open to the day's shortness and viewing it through a new lens made it feel as though much actually had happened, or that I did do a great deal.

I saw kids playing basketball; I saw honeybees bumbling about a tuft of cilantro flowers; I saw a mockingbird and a dove, each atop separate telephone wires, speaking to each other.

I wondered how I would be judged if just today were to be my entire life. Was I being good? Was I being evil? What sort of judgment would be passed on me?

To merely observe the world seemed insufficient. I began to wonder if I could hurl myself into the world . . . do *more* than simply exist.

*   *   *

And so I continued walking about the Island. I saw many people with sunburns and I said hello to them. I felt that one way of feeling at least more relevant was to express more humanity—to be more humane—for as I age I indeed notice that one's sense of humanity can vanish and you wake up one morning feeling not quite as . . . *human* as you once did. So saying hello was a small start in this direction.

Toward sunset I walked toward the harbor, past some large houses, and I got to thinking about how some people are rich in worldly things, and how some people are not, but how silly it seems if life is only a day long. And I thought of all the rich people I know, and how so many of them sit alone in their living rooms saying to themselves, "So . . . what's next?" And I thought of all the not-so-rich people I know, and how desperately they want to be alone inside a cool, clean living room saying, "So . . . what's next?"

I arrived at the harbor just as a tangerine sun was sinking into turquoise waters charged with angel fish and minnows. I watched this from a bench, and an old man who is known locally for telling rambling stories to audiences who would probably rather not listen came up to me and rambled, as he tends to do. Other people walking by gave me knowing looks of sympathy as well as relief at their not being in my situation.

And so this old man and I watched the sun go down and he said that when the Day of Judgment comes, each of us will melt down into the earth, gently and slowly, just as the sun melts down into the ocean. I was startled, as judgment was very much on my mind today. After this, the man left in pursuit of fresher audiences, and I walked home, thinking.

Normally when the sun goes down, the world loses its attractions and I reach for a cocktail the way my hand reaches for the car radio's ON button when the car hits

110 DOUGLAS COUPLAND

a red light. But tonight I didn't, and I decided to pass by the outside patio bar where many people were enjoying rum drinks. I went home and observed the night.

There was heat lightning on the horizon, over in the direction of Nassau, as well as an unusual number of shooting stars. The stars themselves were dense in the sky tonight, like an enormous batik fabric.

Outside my house there was a woman standing beside her bicycle scrutinizing the stars. She pointed out a constellation to me. I thanked her but told her I didn't want to know any constellations. She asked me why, and I told her it was because many years ago I had learned the names of all the plants, and I wanted to at least keep the skies a mystery.

But then she told me she had no choice *but* to learn the constellations. I asked her why, and she said she had two sons who attended school halfway around the world, and so the only common ground they had was the sky.

We said our good-byes and I sat down on my stoop, a lizard scurrying to my right, wasps sleeping in their nest in the rafters outside the bathroom window, and I felt my day coming to an end.

I guess the thing about today is that I spent it alone—not with *you*. Are you the person I'm thinking of right now? Maybe you are. Where are you? Where did you go? The day is fading and I'm wondering about my next life, tomorrow. I wish it was with you.

We all have a "you" in our life . . . someone out there who was to have spent the day with us, but who then went away for some reason. That special "you" is not here now. Nor is the sun inside the green bottles of the graveyard wall, nor is the sun reflecting on the angelfish, now fluttering inside black waters.

The sun has fallen into the world as I have fallen into the world, but the sun will not be judged for falling whereas I will judge myself.

And tomorrow when I rise with a new sun and a new life, I will redeem

_`
Superstock

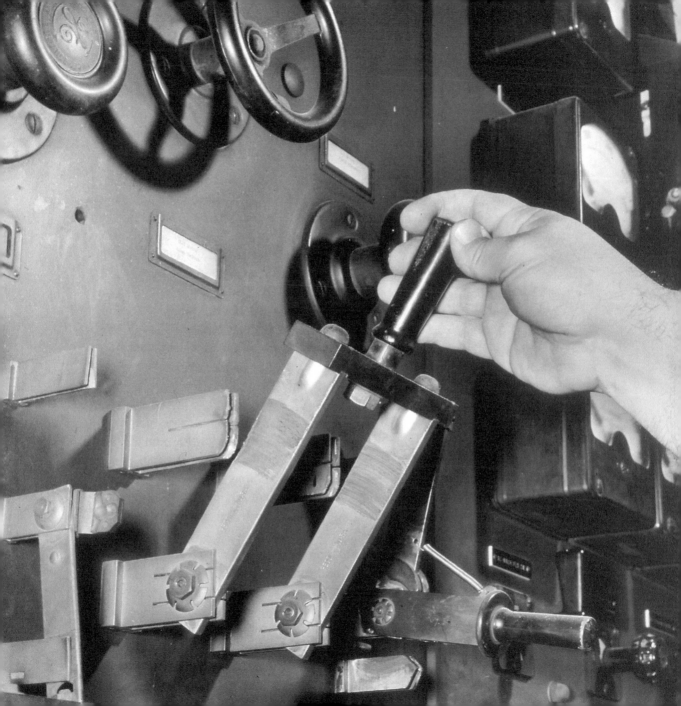

myself and I will find you, and you will be here in my life, and we will walk the Island's roads together.

POSTCARD NUMBER TWO:
POWER FAILURE

I really wonder whether all memories are the same or if some are "more impor- tant" than others. Like many people my age, I was exposed to extreme amounts of well-produced, high-quality information and entertainment from birth onward. The other day I saw a Shake 'n Bake TV commercial, one I had not seen in twenty years, and in a flash, the whole commercial came back to me, as though I had just seen it five minutes ago. So I guess my head is stuffed with an almost-endless series of corporation-sponsored consumer tableaux of various lengths. These "other" commercialized memories are all in my head, somewhere, and this is indeed something worth considering.

What would it be like to have never had these commercialized images in my head? What if I had grown up in the past or in a nonmedia culture? Would I still be "me"? Would my "personality" be different?

I think the unspoken agreement between us as a culture is that we're not sup- posed to consider the commercialized memories in our head as real, that real life consists of time spent away from TVs, magazines and theaters. But soon the planet will be entirely populated by people who have only known a world with TVs and computers. When this point arrives, will we still continue with pre-TV notions of identity? Probably not. Time continues on: Instead of buying blue Chairman Mao outfits, we shop at the Gap. Same thing. Everybody travels everywhere. "Place" is a joke.

And here's something we've all noticed: During power failures we sing songs, but the moment the electricity returns, we atomize.

I am choosing to live my life in a permanent power failure. I look at the screens and glossy pages and I don't let them become memories.

When I meet people, I imagine them in a world of darkness. The only lights that count are the sun, candles, the fireplace and the light inside of you, and if I seem strange to you at times, it's only because I'm switching off the power, trying to help us both, trying to see you and me as the people we really are.

17

POSTCARD FROM
PALO ALTO

PALO ALTO TURNED ONE HUNDRED TODAY. PALO ALTO IS WHERE TV'S BRADY BUNCH would have lived (and still might): amid the Arcadian suburban foliage of the mid–San Francisco Peninsula—in shingled Arts and Crafts neighborhoods flocked by eucalyptus, junipers, pears, tree ferns, sequoias and flowering grapefruits—or in quiet rancher-lined streets bursting with Nile lilies and Watsonia, purple Mexican sage and hibiscus; bright yellow flowering patio daisy trees and clematis vines.

Palo Alto is also home to Hewlett-Packard and hundreds of other Silicon Valley tech firms—each of them also elegantly and discreetly nestled behind precisely bermed and groomed grounds—fully considered landscapes politely serenaded into a sunny lull by the intermittent *tsk-tsk* of sprinklers and the occasional hum of a passing Lexus or giggles of passing youths on bicycles.

Palo Alto (population 55,900) is perhaps the last fully functioning, fiscally secure middle-class California dreamscape in existence. Its twenty-six square miles are a gracious and charming place in which to live, and there are no caveats on enjoyment of the place. It is a lovely city and it works; it has given the world far more than it has ever taken, and to find any fault would be gratuitous and petty. It is the embodiment of middle-class tranquility and freedom. It is Palo Alto, or a platonic vision of a city like this, that lurks in the backs of many minds as the ideal that is worth fighting for when fighting is called for.

Stanford University, Palo Alto's initial engine and raison d'être, was founded in 1891 by railroad tycoon Leyland Stanford in memory of his son, Leyland Jr., who died of cholera during that family's Italian voyage. The mightily endowed campus, like most coastal California campuses, is an abundant collection of terra-cotta-roofed buldings surrounded by well-established, properly tended foliage. As one drives up University Avenue from downtown Palo Alto—the quarter-mile westward to the main quad buildings, sentineled on both sides by beefy, obviously old Canary Island date palms of Mediterranean aspect—one realizes that this is a place blessed with never having had to scrimp.

But quickly enough, in the middle of this palmed drive, off to the left, there is, what seems to be at first glance, a road of a sort one might find in a failed housing subdivision in, say, Georgia or Mississippi: faded macadam crumbling on the sides surrounded by what appears to be . . . nothing. Break away from University Avenue to walk down this road and suddenly, inexplicably, all evidence of maintenance vanishes—all evidence of *humanity* vanishes. We have traveled back in time a million years. Where are we?

This is the Arboretum Restoration Project to preserve marsh and restore oaks. The grass isn't mown here—it is an experiment in anti-landscaping: to restore what once *was*. Wear thick pants if you visit—the oatlike grass is dense with last year's dead brown thistles, brambles, fan palms, orange California poppies and skinny fractal-shaped skeletons of some sort of plant that is, for the moment, out of season but seems to grow quickly enough when in season. There are adolescent oaks, swampy patches, ant holes and chatting birds. A myriad of plants, many of them rare, are tiny but lush in April, and will soon render the landscape almost impenetrable.

The overall feel on today is prehistoric. There is a mood of dilophosauri and raptors lurking hungrily in the oak copses—of the savagery that lurks to recapture even the most Disneyfied of environments in the absence of vigilance. This is a landscape in which nature is being allowed to recreate the complexities inherent in the wild. The sounds of engines in the near distance fail to reassure.

From within the Arboretum, the only manmade structure visible, and then barely, is just above the trees off to the southwest, a campanile. One heads toward it, and soon enough one is out of the paleo-landscape and into a youthscape of volleyball, Rollerbladers, sunburned coeds and Hondas.

The campanile is the carillon tower of the Herbert Hoover Institute on War, Revolution and Peace, founded in 1941 by Hoover, a Palo Altan. In the piazza fountain outside the building's main entrance, frat kids slosh one another with gobs of water scooped with Frisbees. Inside the tower's main doors, the atmosphere instantly becomes diametrically sober. To the right is a somber oil portrait of the somber Hoover.

On either side of an almost parodically grim 1940s information booth in the cool, echoey antechamber, are two museum rooms, one on the left dedicated to Hoover's wife, Lou Henry Hoover, and one on the right to Hoover himself. One feels as if one has accidentally strayed into an offbeat museum after having a flat tire in a strange town—like a "Museum of Walnuts," say, or "Life with Manganese."

Hoover's room is the size of a 7-Eleven but with high, cool stone walls. Waist-high glass display cases around the room's edge offer fragments of Hooveriana such as a chunk of Hematite ore collected by Hoover in Kalgoorlie, Australia, in 1912, and bits of Belgian lace—rewards from Hoover-organized World War I relief efforts. There is a 1921 letter, approved by Lenin, from Maxim Gorky to the West, pleading for aid for the starving Russian people. On a 24-inch Sony there is a haunting five-minute loop of black-and-white footage of Hoover himself, declaring that the institute and the 1.2 million documents it houses "aid in the development of makers of peace."

In the center of the room is a vitrine containing a pewter model of the Hoover Dam and a small cast-iron sculpture titled *Tolstoy and Plow*, by Solovieva, in honor of Hoover's reorganization of the Kyshtyn iron mine in 1910. And at the end of the display is a wall-mounted copy of Hoover's 1941 book, *The Problems of Lasting Peace*. Time and memory may not have been overly generous with Hoover, but there is no denying the essential fine intentions of the man—intentions bred in Palo Alto.

For a dollar one can ascend to the fourteenth-floor tower, the only manmade sight-seeing spot in the entire Silicon Valley. One is informed that the gentleman who once operated the tower's carillon has retired, and that the bells play only rarely now, the last time being the 1992 visit to Stanford of Mikhail Gorbachev.

It is a beautiful day, and the view is staggering. To the north are San Francisco and the bridges of the Bay. To the south are San Jose, Santa Clara, Sunnyvale, Cupertino, Mountain View and other cities—the forges of the post–industrial age housed in their industrial parks and flanked by Palo Alto–ish suburbs whose well-considered greenery almost visibly pump oxygen into the blue sky of this fine spring day.

To the west is the campus—Rodin's *Thinker* in the library quad below and the spiney mountain of the Peninsula some miles away. And to the east lies the other side of the campus from where whooping noises from the stadium are carried upward in the wind. And past the campus is the city of Palo Alto itself.

Palo Alto—one hundred years old. Palo Alto, dreaming of peace, dreaming of the day it will have its ten thousandth birthday, quietly knowing that peace is not the natural state of the world, that the world is actually more like Jurassic Park, a patch of which the university maintains in the form of the Arboretum Restoration land, clearly visible from Herbert Hoover's bell tower, like a seed lying in dormancy—a seed that may or may never germinate, depending entirely on the will of the people.

Palo Alto, California
April 16, 1994

18

JAMES ROSENQUIST'S
F-111

(F-ONE ELEVEN)

IMAGINE LIVING ON THE EDGE OF THE WORLD (VANCOUVER) AND ATTENDING A SMALL elementary school in a remote suburb next to a forest, beyond which there is nothing except forest and alps and tundra and ice for thousands of miles until the North Pole, which is, in itself, nothing in particular. Next stop after that: literally, Siberia.

Imagine the year is 1970 and you are eight years old. Imagine that you have no religion. Imagine that the houses lived in by you and your friends are all built by contractors and furnished with dreams provided by *Life* magazine. Imagine that you inhabit a world with no history and no ideology.

Imagine then attending this elementary school on the edge of the world and opening a copy of the encyclopedia and finding under Art, a long, thin panel of a certain painting: *F-111* (pronounced eff-one-eleven). It contains, among others, images of an angel food cake, tinned spaghetti, the words "U.S. AIR FORCE," a nuclear explosion, and a Firestone tire, all splashed across the length of an F-111 fighter plane. All of these images are painted in shocking, bright colors—all of these images that flow daily inside your head—images now all recontextualized in a seductive, validated World Book-ified context. [Fun fact: My computer's grammar-check function tells me to "avoid jargon words like "RECONTEXTU-ALIZED." And right it is!] There is even a young girl, roughly your own age, underneath a hair dryer. In all probability, she has her own ABC *Afterschool Special*.

Epiphany.

Warhol (another art discovery I made shortly after I discovered Rosenquist) said that once you saw the world as Pop, you could never look at it the same way ever again. Absolutely true. Early family memory: Young Douglas cutting up *Life* magazines bought for twenty-five cents apiece at a local secondhand book store and pasting fragments of pictures together—making "Rosenquists" while annoying his brothers, baffling his parents. Ahhh . . . a vision of postmodernism.

We emerge from our mother's womb an unformatted diskette; our culture formats us.

The best *Life* magazine years for Rosenquist-style montages were from about 1948 to 1962. That's when the imagery was at its most generic—its Sears Roebuck-iest—when guns and butter were roaring ahead full blast. In 1955 it was not an issue for Hormel or Van Kamp's to spend X-thousand dollars to show a full-page photo of ham.

I remember bowls of Campbell's vegetable soup; beach balls; astronauts;

swing sets; wood-paneled station wagons. Yet even by 1970 it all seemed some-what extreme. But it was big and sexy and full of money—Pop!—and best of all, it was *generic*. The generic postulates an ideal—something that was, if not miss-ing, then rather beside the point on the edge of the world in 1970.

These *Life*-ish images are now, of course, the images that have come to define the probably-never-existed-anyway ironic norm of Cold War Boom culture: Dad smoking a pipe; Mom in an apron. It's beyond a joke. It's no longer even worth being ironic about. And, as irony itself seems to be on shaky ground these days, ironists, seeking ever more obscure tactics, need pooh-pooh the clumsier, more puppy-like ironic thrusts of early Pop. This, of course, makes necessary a revision of Pop. *Was* Pop ironic? Was Andy *all* irony? Was Rosenquist ever at *all* ironic? *Who* was sincere . . . if at all? And which artists will emerge from this neo-Marxist theorizing intact?

It's nearing twenty-five years since I first saw *F-111* and I have never actually seen it in real life. I have seen it only, in varying sizes and gatefolds, in books and magazines. Trying to imagine its size and luxuriousness is a part of the experi-ence. It's always amusing to see the way in which magazines and books try to deal with the painting's awkward dimensions. Other Rosenquist paintings I have seen in person—the earlier ones—have surprised me with their guckiness: masking tape ripped away revealing unclean lines; dribbles; muck. Only Rosenquist's later works have the seamlessness the earlier works seemed to have been dreaming of.

Rosenquist was always the hardest Pop painter to find information on. I remember once locating a photo of New York's art-collecting Scull family (Warhol immor-talized its matron, Ethel, in the portrait, *Ethel Scull 36 Times*) eating dinner in front of a Rosenquist painting titled *Silver Skies* (more Firestone tires plus a goose's head)—a painting located in the Scull family's dining room. Their *dining room*. I thought to myself, "This is a family that does *not* live next to the wilderness. Who *is* this family? What do they *believe* in? Do they have religion? And on Sundays, do Mr. and Mrs. Scull take the kids out to see *F-111*? And afterward do the Sculls lunch at Le Cirque with the girl under the *F-111*'s hairdryer (and her agent)?"

If you look at the work of the Pop artists, much of it seems to be contemplating some future day when human ideas can be more readily mediated by machines. The painstaking mid-sixties graphics of Tadonori Yokoo now seem like the template from which most computerized graphic design (in Asia, at least) is drawn. Jasper Johns's and Robert Rauschenberg's muckiest creations scream Photo Shop software; Warhol is a pure endorsement of the color laser printer twenty-five years in advance.

    Last December I was in San Francisco, at a digital animation studio. While talking with a producer there, we got to discussing our favorite artists, and Rosenquist's name came up. I said that someday I would like to do a Rosenquist Simulator—a PC-TV product that cuts, pastes, fades and dissolves whatever non-text TV channels are on at any given moment—in order to generate an endless, living Rosenquist for the living room wall. He said it would not, actually, be a difficult thing to do.

Much of my faith in the future—*most* of my faith in the future—was invested, however wittingly, in the world of art, and Modern art at that. It was through art that I ultimately came to learn that no history is, in itself, history—possibly its most liberating and uncruel form. (You sentimentalize bourgeois consumption patterns; you must be punished.)

I think all the Pop artists loved the subjects they painted. Detachment, what there was of it, was a put-on. *F-111* is one of the largest antiwar paintings ever created. Pop artists loved the machine that formatted the diskette that was them. *F-111* says to me, "Love the machine that formatted the diskette that is *you*."

    Culture ho.

19

POSTCARD FROM
LOS ALAMOS

(ACID CANYON)

THE LOCAL OLDIES STATION, KBOM 106.7 ("WE DON'T GLOW, BUT WE'RE RADIOAC-tive!") plays Peter Frampton's "Do You Feel Like We Do?" as we skim over a chewing-gum pink road built of gravel hewn from nearby *Bugs Bunny–Road Runner Hour*–like mesas. Climbing the steep grade of New Mexico Route 502, we pass an unmarked white eighteen-wheeler sandwiched front and back by pairs of Chevy Suburbans with blacked-out windows. The Suburbans are a miniplex of antennas, dishes and wires; communications between all five vehicles crackle almost visibly, like Van de Graaff generator sparks. The bodyguarded eighteen-wheeler is headed up Pueblo Canyon to the Los Alamos National Laboratory; it is carrying a load of, well . . . er . . . (*insert the name of something extremely frightening here*).

Los Alamos, population 18,000, eighty miles north of Albuquerque, is a must-see destination for the small, emerging dedicated band of nuclear tourists. It is a defense-contracting-based town, home of the Los Alamos National Laboratory, which is managed by the University of California (five-year contract recently renewed). It has to its credit, among an extraordinary number of other nuclear inventions, the mixed honor of being the place where the first atomic bomb was assembled. It is part of a travel menu that also includes the fabled Doomtowns of the Nevada test site, the aging plutonium production culture of Hanford, Washington's tri-city region (Richland/Pasco/Kennewick), the Missile Garden of Alamogordo, New Mexico, and the Trinity Site, near Alamogordo, home of the world's first nuclear detonation.

Los Alamos's main nuclear tourist destination is the Los Alamos Sales Company—probably the world's only dealer in what owner Ed Grothus calls "nuclear waste." (In fact, it sells non-radioactive cast-offs from the laboratory.) Set atop a lovely hill tufted with ponderosa pines and junipers, the company is housed in two structures: an A-frame building that was once a Missouri Synod Lutheran church, and a small supermarket, the Shop 'n' Cart, that went out of business in 1985.

To tour through the Black Hole, Grothus's affectionate nickname for his facility, is to take a tour through a land of dead technologies and dead ideology. Old grocery-era signage still hangs from the supermarket's sagging, water-stained ceiling. Aisle 2: soap, bleach, detergents, fabric softener, dog food, cat food. The aisle now contains a jumble of dusty petri dishes, O-rings, microphones, augers, liquefied gas dewars, bins of bulk resistors, pre-amps, glass piping, vacuum jars and -o-meters of all sorts.

In the church there are four Noguchi-sculpture-ish pod lights hanging from the ceiling's apex. The pulpit is stuffed, helter skelter, with dead adding machines and attenuators. Where pews once sat lies a Toyota-sized linguine of black multi-pair cables. The structure is full to overflowing with the chassis of ammeters, DC voltmeters, microfiche reading machines, thermocouples and paper-tape punch-control devices. Broken radio tubes, lost SHIFT keys, wire fragments, number plates, transistors, small springs, patches of rust and cogs litter the floor. Honeywell seems to have done very well by Los Alamos. Ditto Union Carbide, Polaroid and Eastman Kodak. Some of the products and their names and makers have an almost touching, dated, extinct or nearly extinct feel to them:

> a vaporizer by Chryo-Chem Inc., of Carson, California
> a Heiland Strobonar 91B
> a single-phase insulated transformer by the Square D Co. of Milwaukee, Wisconsin
> a Racal-Vadic VA3434
> a DT-360 from the Data Technology Corp.

Near a rear door, covered in pine needles, there is a December 1975 issue of *Datamation* magazine; a closeby date book is opened to September 23, 1980, as if that was the day, in a science-fiction movie, on which time came to an end.

Los Alamos, like most other defense-based civic economies, is searching for ways in which to repurpose itself. And as with so many other Cold War–era tech towns, its mood is reflexively conservative. President Clinton's 1993 swords-to-plow-shares speech in Los Alamos met with tepid response. As Ed Grothus says, "Everybody turned out, but Los Alamos isn't Clinton country." Santa Fe, thirty-five miles to the south, is looked on as an ideological and perhaps economic threat. New Age is pronounced "newage," to rhyme with *sewage*. The joke *du jour* is, Q: Why did the Santa Fean cross the street? A: He was channeling a chicken.

Though the city's Chamber of Commerce 1994 *Visitor's Guide* pitches the post–Cold War Los Alamos as a superior recreation and tourism destination, the city exudes denial. It has the time-stunted feel of having been constructed some-time between the Rosenberg trial and the year *Bewitched* went off the air. Street names include: Kristi Lane, Scott Way and Tiffany Court. There is virtually no architectural evidence of the 1980s in Los Alamos or even the late 1970s. There does exist, however, an aura of low-grade, Pynchonesque paranoia. Local high school kids speak easily of "Acid Canyon," a nearby locale where toxics were allegedly dumped, and of brain cancer and leukemia clusters. Cub Scout merit badges apparently once touted mushroom clouds.

But change is happening quickly in Los Alamos. Ed Grothus, now seventy years old, is beginning a liquidation process of his inventory so that he can pursue other interests, most notably a Museum of the Nuclear Age, filled with the best of what he has salvaged over the past forty years.

And the local newspapers have been flooded with news from Energy Secretary Hazel O'Leary's openness initiative. In recently disclosed Los Alamos experiments of the 1950s and 1960s, people, children included, swallowed or breathed radioactive materials so scientists could study the absorption of those materials into the body: iodine in the thyroid and encapsulated radioactive uranium and manganese in the intestinal tract, and dinners of radioactive zinc, tritium and cesium. And the machines that manufactured and created these capsules, powders, broths and solutions—all of these dreadful snacks—now sit quietly, with great probability, somewhere inside the Black Hole, covered in dust and perlite, locked forever in a sort of *Our Town*–ish death-dream, a dream of McCarthyist rants, of tract housing, of dogs in orbit and of that one bright light that made so much forgetting possible.

20

WASHINGTON, D.C.: FOUR MICROSTORIES, SUPER TUESDAY 1992

01 EVERYBODY HAS AIDS

Mark Reinstein/FPG

KYLE LOVES THE SMELL OF HIS INDEX FINGER. HE SNIFFS IT AS HE LOVE-TAPS HIS JEEP into the Taurus with diplomatic plates parked behind him.

"I call this parking by ear," he tells Laura, who's already reaching for her door handle with her right hand, her black leather attaché case clutched tensely in her left. "Hey," Kyle continues, "I should try and get Detroit lobbying for spikes welded onto bumpers. Whaddya think, Laur?"

"I think, good *night*, Kyle." Laura swings a leg over the door sill, visibly itching to escape into her shared studio suite in the Georgetown brownstone, a spit away. To her alarm, Kyle turns off the ignition.

"Boy, am I glad we ditched that dinner hole, Laur. Was it Mars-Needs-Women, or what?" Kyle is refering to their recently departed dinner spot, an empty-ish yuppie hell off Dupont Circle. The food was misspelled French, entertainment a sullen trio of unemployed Czech claymation artists listlessly tweaking out "Ode to Joy" on the rims of partially filled brandy snifters. Kyle, a political marketing consultant and the son of Laura's father's partner from back home in Yell County, Texas, also provided entertainment during dinner by showing Laura a wad of fifties converted with a felt pen into a flip movie of copulating lizards. "We give out these bills to focus-group members," Kyle said of the money rippling through his fingers. "Believe *me*, the focus-group fifty is the true fuel in the engine of consumer democracy."

Laura said, "*Char*ming," and retreated into her morally superior haze. Laura, a twenty-two-year-old Williams College poli-sci grad earning 17K as krill on the food chain of her local senator's office, cannot afford to be righteous. She finds Kyle's amorality loathsome. For example, during dinner she questioned the freshness of her tarragon-sauced capon. "Mob-supplied, no doubt," she said, picking apart its tendons. "Why doesn't the government clamp down on the Mafia more? If nothing else, they're a health menace."

"Hey, hon," replied Kyle, "the Feds hate the mob because the mob doesn't pay taxes, not because it's evil. But your sentimentality is sweet." Kyle then vacuumed a snail from its coil and smiled at Laura: "You know, Laura Warshawski, George Washington was Polish and had red hair, just like *you*. I suppose democracy must be in your genes."

Kyle then went on to describe his company's pursuit of photo opportunities for a new client, a multiple-incumbency senator on career thin ice over bimbette speculations. "You know the usual: coffee klatches in aerospace factory cafeterias cooing. . . with crack babies . . . snapping baseball-cap adjuster straps with bankrupt sorghum farmers. You'd be amazed at the frequent-flyer points I'm racking up. *Ooh* . . . check out the dessert wagon."

Now, outside of Laura's brownstone, their "date" is nearly over. The self-conscious good manners that silenced Laura up to now are temporarily shelved as she stands in a bouquet of litter beside the curb and motions Kyle to stay in his vehicle. She pauses; now is a chance for her to score a point. "Hey, Kyle, just tell me this: is there anything you believe in? One thing? *Anything?*"

"Believe?" asks Kyle, like a Santa speeking to a child at the mall, and leaning over roguishly as he grabs for Laura's hand.

"You know"—Laura holds Kyle's hand sternly, like a mother teaching a naughty child a lesson—"something you'd *fight* for. Something you'd place before yourself."

"Such as?"

"Such as better education . . . health care . . . lobbying for shelter for the homeless . . . lobbying for research for people with AIDS . . ." Laura realizes as she speaks that she is enjoying the surprisingly rough texture of Kyle's palm and the way he gently strokes the underside of her wrist with his odorous index digit. She is surprised when he then suddenly breaks the clasp, laughs, and pulls back into the Jeep.

He turns the key and the engine makes a grinding noise; Kyle makes a sour apple face, reignites the engine and says to Laura, "Lobby-lobby-*lobby*. Hon, you're new to D.C. Such a puppy. Phone me in ten years."

He pops the stereo button, releasing an explosion of Metallica and says to Laura, under the music's blare in a thoughtfully out-of-character manner before hurtling out onto Wisconsin Avenue, "Hon, *every*body has AIDS."

02 MONEY IS ENERGY

Tim is a smart young fellow with a high IQ. Well, *actually*, Tim has never taken a real IQ test. Rather, this morning riding in from Fairfax, he completed the self-score IQ test in an *Omni* magazine. And he cheated. But nevertheless, Tim is a smart fellow.

Tim specializes as a vulnerability consultant. If you are an aspiring politician, you hire Tim, who pretends he is the *National Enquirer*. He researches into your past and locates your "sensitive spots": that joint you smoked in the eleventh grade; your daughter who runs with a bike gang; the fling you flung in Sacramento during that endless plenary weekend. For an extra fee, Tim will help you spin these soft spots.

Like most consultants profiting from the burgeoning world of political technology, Tim worships the database. He knows how to narrowcast information into persuadable sectors of what he calls the "simian population base;" he can merge TV-viewing databases with voting databases. He is proud not to be just another twenty-eight-year-old burnout case from the Hill.

Tim's work is varied. For instance, this morning back at the cinder-block office in Virginia, he earned $1,500 helping yet one more telegenic candidate increase his T.V.Q. rating. Inside the TelePrompTer-equipped simulation TV studio, Tim counseled "Mr. Leadership" (the in-office joke name for all candidates) on the ins and outs of televised speaking. "Energy! Energy!" he hissed into the control booth mike. Now Tim's voice is scratchy.

Afterward, around noon, as Tim was leaving the office for D.C., Shawna at the reception desk expressed minor worries that "the whole voting thing" and the movies were becoming identical processes.

"Well, in that case," replied Tim, "there's only one thing to do."

"What's that?" asked Shawna.

"Go see more movies."

So Tim took his own advice; he blew off an afternoon seminar and instead caught a matinee of *Fantasia*.

Now, just afterward, following a brief stroll, he is standing on a curb on New Hampshire Avenue where, mildly drugged by *Fantasia*'s beauty and by nutritionless nine-plex food, he tries to flag a taxi. Beside him, roped off by yellow strands of plastic safety taping, are three rusty-orange mounds of soil dug up by road crews replacing sewage pipes. The workmen have temporarily vanished, but Tim sees the tools they have left behind, jabbing into the three conical piles of exhumed earth, which glow like amber in the late-afternoon sun—earth originally dug up hundreds of years ago during the birth of the nation, then reburied once more.

Tim peeks into the soil more closely, looking for bottles and other antique junk. He remembers an interview he has scheduled for tomorrow in Manassas, Virginia, with an impoverished ex-mistress of a certain senator, and makes a quick note of the meeting on his pocket Aiwa recorder.

Patting the recorder in his chest pocket, Tim resumes his search into the exhumed Washington soil, the soil from beneath the city, picking out from amid the rusted sewage pipes the objects that may or may not be encaked in guck: old garbage; maybe an old shoe; rotting telephones; decayed inventions; the things from our past; the things we thought were transient; and best of all, maybe a few coins.

03
OBEDIENCE
ISN'T
A
VIRTUE

Matthew shaved his head bald in order to express solidarity with his friend, Chester, who began chemotherapy four days ago and who is shortly scheduled to lose all of his hair. Chester was untalented enough to develop stomach cancer without having medical insurance, and now lolls about a Bethesda, Maryland, hospital room drinking barium sulfate goo cut with Nestlé Quik while contemplating his imminent eviction from the hospital.

The normally apathetic Matthew, aside from shaving his head bald in sympathy, has also made another change in his life because of Chester's medical crisis— he has decided to help work on a local primary campaign. This decision came about in the following way: Matthew had been having a jolly good gripe-fest on the phone to Chester about the White House and the whole uncaring cash-o-centric system.

After a lengthy pause at the conclusion of Matthew's rant, Chester, silent on

Nestlé

Quik®

Real Chocolate
Flavor

NET WT 16 OZ (1 LB) (454g)

the other end of the line in Bethesda, said, "Okay then, Mr. Sit-on-Your-Ass, keep slacking around waiting to invent the perfect unified theory to cure all the country's ills. Meanwhile the real world turns to shit. And hey, here's a suggestion— why not go out and do something genuinely political for once—okay, *dude*? Because, like, my own time appears to be limited now, and whining like yours doesn't seem to cut it anymore. Anyway, I've got an enema in five minutes and I need that time to adjust my attitude. Later."

Click.

Matthew can understand why Chester has become so no-nonsense since the diagnosis. Now Matthew rubs his prickly cranium, voluntarily employed in the temporary field office of a presidential-primary candidate, a stab at involvement, housed in a bankrupt furniture store sandwiched between a Sock Shop and a steakhouse in a suburban Rockville, Maryland, shopping mall. Surrounding Matthew are Samsung PC monitors atop folding tables, megaphones, confused pastas of telephone cords, strips of dot-matrix paper trim and the claustrophobic odor of weak coffee. Above him is a felt-penned poster saying DON'T STAPLE SIGNS TO TREES.

When Matthew arrived at the field office a few days ago, the organizers in charge, young men of strangely cultish energy and enthusiastic indoor wearers of sunglasses, took one glance at Matthew's hairlessness, his ripped jeans and his VISU-ALIZE IMPEACHMENT T-shirt, and plopped him ignominiously in the rear of the office.

"You can help monitor the visibility," he was told by a Nautilized office organizer named HI I'M BROCK in the standard-issue navy three-piece suit of young ambitious people.

"Visibility?"

"Lawn signs," said HI I'M BROCK, pointing to an unloved-looking stack of pine sticks and cardboard signboards touting sloganistic piffle.

Matthew was then left to fend for himself at his assigned post, next to the chainsmoking Grace, a veteran of a half-dozen campaigns, who was outlining a map of the Maryland panhandle with a bingo marker, and who told him consolingly, "Lawn signs aren't much work these days. TV wiped 'em out. Kids toss 'em into the gullies, anyway"—short pause—"can I touch your head?"

Near the office front sit the young political workers who are more willing to give convincing simulations of political behavior. There, in front of dirt- and sun-streaked windows, Matthew sees the no-grief-in-their-lives twenty-one-year-olds eagerly building a political component into their résumés; he sees the scruffy New York–based phone junkies who Amtrak-ed to Maryland from New Hampshire; he sees the suit-and-Ray-Ban boys gladhanding the local visiting politicos; he sees high school kids idly parroting their parents' jingoism as they collate 8½-by-11 candidate-statement sheets.

In the rear of the office Matthew has quickly fallen into his own mindless sleepy rhythm and is contemptuous but bemused at how quickly his attempts at democratic participation have decayed into pointlessness. Occasionally he is spoken to hurriedly by one of the young Ray-Ban types who need to know about a load of signs going to Wicomico or Anne Arundel counties. At any moment Matthew expects Grace to confide in him her experiences as a UFO abductee—or offer him another shelf-life treat from her desktop collection culled mainly from the Circle K. But mostly Matthew is forgotten.

Into his third day Matthew phones Chester and offers a progress report. "Hey, Chess, I'm trying, but it's kind of goofy and pointless here. When you think about it, though, there's not much else you can do to participate in politics these days. Any fresh ideas?"

"Well, dude, the system can't remain monolithic forever. It's gotta change somewhere. Just look at those clever Russians."

"I don't know, Chess. Two identical parties competing against each other with no alternatives—it's like the Disney version of democracy. How do you fight a cartoon?"

Matthew yawns. He had trouble sleeping last night worrying about Chester—plus his own student loans and his so-far fruitless job search. Strange, he thinks, how all the old tricks of success in the world—education, a broad skill base, literacy, numeracy—are no longer guarantees of anything. Also, this morning Matthew skipped breakfast and for lunch ate only a Snapple. So this afternoon in particular, Matthew is feeling tired. After his phone call with Chester ends, he pushes back his chair and closes his eyes.

His stomach growls; his chin digs into his sternum and he tumbles into a daydream. He remembers a story he used to read when he was young, a story in which children were lost in the White House after being separated from a tour—children walking through the building's corridors, dark and quiet. Occasionally Matthew is snapped out of this reverie by voices calling across the office: "Drive-time on the Chesapeake Bridge, 6,000 cars-per-hour, so let's rig up the sign!" and "We need crowd-building action—the Channel Eleven mobile van's arriving at the farmer's rally at three."

But Matthew soon returns to the same childhood story in his thoughts: the lone children walking up steep stairs, wondering where the president is, peeking through ajar doors, their footsteps muffled on deep carpets.

When Matthew was younger he remembered the children were trying to find an escape from the White House—that was the plot of the story—*escaping*. But now in Matthew's head, the children are no longer trying to get out. Rather, they are digging deeper into the silent structure of the White House, behind its gilt trimmings, into its walls paneled in wood, into its walls thick with mirrors and surveillance wires. The children are holding candles now, and flashlights and tools, forcing open locked doors, punching holes through walls and cutting through locks. Looking for food.

04
OUR
CAPACITY
FOR
AMNESIA
IS
TERRIFYING

Juanita has left the TV news office early this afternoon, bored with manufactured news about manufactured candidates. It's spring! She wants to spend part of the day playing tacky tourist—walking the Washington Mall and inspecting the monuments. And she does so to the interior soundtrack of her mother's ambitious Spanish voice always urging her to push, to advance herself, to make sure Juanita doesn't end up as *she* did. This spice of guilt enhances the stolen afternoon. Juanita removes her blazer and drapes it over her shoulder.

Such a country. Juanita remembers first arriving here at age eight, suffocating underneath a trailerload of red bell peppers crossing the Arizona border at Nogales. She remembers later that same day eating a lemon Popsicle in a drugstore and seeing a woman with a blond beehive wig and an A-line dress stroll down the store's clean quiet aisles. She remembers purebred dogs and racks of dolls and signs selling cocktails. She remembers a gang of skateboarders outside the mall who taught her her first English word, which was "cool."

Even then she was surprised at the effortlessness of her new citizenship, which required only a dash of enthusiasm and the act of simply being there. And she has never forgotten this simplicity—and the calm abundance that nourishes its roots—the air conditioning, an aisle of pet food, the cool blonde.

Two decades and a Stanford MBA later, Juanita watches joggers pass the reflecting pool between the Lincoln Memorial and the Washington Monument. She catches fragments of what the joggers are saying—the usual: "What's wrong with the country is the way people don't really care." Blah blah *blah*.

As a new anchor, Juanita can't help but notice slightly more of this chatter about some type of national malaise floating about the air. Perhaps *every* election year is like this. And, being in TV, Juanita knows that certain people have much to gain by propagating such negative discussion.

But yet Juanita detects something else surfacing in people's discussions these days—a worry that something unnameable yet valuable is being forgotten—a knowledge of the formula for the invisible glue that holds the nation together, that keeps the nation from shattering apart.

This glue—what is its recipe? The songs we sang as children? The pictures of founding fathers that adorned our classroom walls? The need to buy and sell real estate? Florida holidays? Campbell's soup? Mobile homes? It is as though the

Mark Reinstein/FPG

nation feels itself to be on the brink of some mass amnesia and is frightened by this very capacity for forgetfulness.

But this discussion tends to be overly intellectualized for Juanita. She just cannot feel the loss her fellow citizens seem to be feeling. She has felt American from the moment she bit into that lemon Popsicle in Nogales and she wonders how it is that such an easy and wonderful sensation as US citizenship can be so simply forgotten—like forgetting your sex.

She walks over the grass, still unmown so early in the year, over to the Vietnam Veterans Memorial, to the black marble V carved into the lawn. Clichéd but true how one can live in a city for years and never see those things that even the most transient of tourists will see.

Juanita admires the Vietnam monument's simplicity and joins the lines of people walking back and forth across its face. She tunes out the buzz, which may or may not be people recognizing her face from the *News at Six*. She stopped noticing *that* long ago. Instead she focuses on the names carved in marble—American names like those of the boys at Stanford, CHRIS and DONALD and SCOTT and NORMAN. She traces out some of the letters with her precisely manicured and varnished nails. At her feet lie bouquets of roses, offerings of unfired fireworks and never-to-be-opened small parcels wrapped in American flags.

A hand taps her shoulder. Juanita turns around to meet an elderly woman wearing tan slacks, her hair in curlers under a red scarf. She is carrying a small bundle of blue carnations. She says to Juanita, "I know you. You're the TV lady."

Juanita says, "Hello," nods politely, and returns her gaze to the black marble. But the woman taps her again and says, "I want you to have a flower, TV lady." And so Juanita accepts a flower from the woman, who is then clasped around the shoulders by a younger woman, visibly her daughter, who makes apologies to Juanita with her eyebrows. After a moment the daughter steers her mother farther down along the monument's face.

Juanita watches the pair, and quietly moves down the slight slope toward them, to the apex of the monument's V. There, Juanita sees the older woman touching the stone with her hands, no doubt rubbing the name of her son carved there. Moved, Juanita ambles closer, whereupon she hears the daughter say, "Mom—stop playing with your reflection. David's name is up here. Mom— David's name is up *here*."

"Oh," says the older woman. "Who's David?"

Part Three

Brentwood Notebook
A Day in the Life
AUGUST 4, 1994

We are born, so to speak, provisionally, it doesn't matter where.
It is only gradually that we compose within ourselves our true
place of origin so that we may be born there retrospectively and
each day more definitely.

—*Rainer Maria Rilke*

MORNING

BRENTWOOD, CALIFORNIA, POPULATION 35,798, IS THE LOS ANGELES DISTRICT where Marilyn Monroe's ambiguously debated death occurred thirty-two years previously in the early evening hours of August 4, 1962. Brentwood is also the psychic nexus of the O. J. Simpson/Nicole Brown saga, somewhere between 10:00 P.M. and 11:00 P.M., June 12, 1994.

Brentwood does not exist. Not technically. It is a hilly, canyoned Los Angeles suburb—a ZIP code: 90049. Letters sent to Brentwood will be returned to sender. Roughly 250 letters a day end up in the small, Northern California town of Brentwood, ZIP code 94513.

Brentwood could have transcended mere 90049 ZIP code-ness and had genuine civic autonomy had it not been for the simple fact of water.

In June of 1916 Brentwood signed a pact with the City of Los Angeles, receiving freshly imported 250-mile Owens aqueduct water courtesy of William Mulholland, in return for incorporation. Brentwood's property values increased and the city gained almost 50 square miles of new territory. Beverly Hills and Santa Monica avoided this pact by virtue of their having enough well water to resist enshackling by Los Angeles.

In the daytime, Brentwood is almost exclusively a city of women old and young, focused on a small band of retail strip along San Vicente Boulevard. There are women peppered with hunky aspiring actors and slinky actresses springing about from auditions to the gym. It is a soap opera terrarium of post-humanized objects of desire pantherishly unleashed into the boudoir. The worker bees are across Interstate 405 in the city, or in Santa Monica or in the Valley—at ARCO, Disney, The Prudential, Security Bank, RAND, Lorimar, UCLA and the Jon Douglas Realtors Company. Brentwood gives the impression of being a 1970s future utopia, one with a secret at its core, perhaps a pleasant secret and perhaps an unpleasant secret, but a secret that nonetheless remains fiercely protected. Brentwood, like Palm Springs, offers a version of an alternative future that might have occurred had certain factors not continued unchecked, futures that daily seem less probable.

Brentwood generates a mood that arises, possibly, from the difference between what Brentwood posits itself as being (a secular nirvana: better living through sex, money, fame and infrastructure) and what the suburb actually is. One receives the distinct aura of a municipality embodying secularism in crisis. And a part of the crisis of secularity seems to stem from a crisis in our cultural concept of fame, the body—and the way we dream of leading our lives. The area possesses an air of exile: Bermuda during the 1940s; the duke of Windsor, half-crazed with boredom. The unsolved murder of Harry Oakes. During its early years, it was a suburb somewhat engaged in Anglophilia.

Five miles eastward down Santa Monica Boulevard stand the twin towers of the ABC Entertainment Center at Century City. These towers, plus the ocean's presence to the west, combined with the Santa Monica Mountain Range canyons, lend Brentwood a notion of geographical "place-ishness."

> **Q:** What sort of person lives in Brentwood? Old money? New? Offshore? Midwest spinsters? Middle-class aerospaceoids holding on to their jobs by their teeth? Hungry young TriStar execs? Angie Dickinson? Divorcées? Poverty line pensioners? Gym freaks? Soap opera walk-ons?
>
> **A:** All of the above.

Brentwood is not a place where one establishes a dynastic root. It is not a homestead neighborhood. North American suburbs rarely are places where people expect their children to inherit the family Tara. Traditionally people came to Brentwood to raise families, with the common end scenario being divorce, atomization, property divestiture and a move onward. This is the way it works in suburbs; Brentwood is no exception: the kids grow up and leave; the parents move to Newport or Santa Barbara or Connecticut.

Families come and go. Increasingly Brentwood is a district of diatomic professional couples earning large incomes. The household molecules are growing increasingly smaller, richer and older. It's no longer a place where one goes to breed Bradys.

One learns that Bel Air, Hollywood and the Canyons used to be the only "talent-sided" neighborhoods. In recent years, the talent has moved in greater numbers to Brentwood, in pursuit of invisibility, in pursuit of privacy.

Confessional wisdom has it that "Mediterranean" is the sort of house where the "talent" likes to live. Writers and production people prefer Tudor-style houses, remnants of L.A.'s turn-of-the-century Anglophilia.

*   *   *

HONORARY MAYORS OF BRENTWOOD

(8-by-10-inch glossies on view at the First Interstate Bank, 11836 San Vicente)

1968	Lloyd Nolan
1970	Fred MacMurray
1971	Phyllis Diller
1974	Lorne Greene
1976	Sandy Duncan
1978	John Forsythe
1981	Tony Franciosa
1985	Mark Harmon
1986	John Saxon
1992	Sally Struthers

Celebrities Who Live/d Within O. J. Simpson's 460-House Brentwood Park Neighborhood

Julie Andrews, Roseanne, Gary Cooper, Joan Crawford, Angie Dickinson, Phyllis Diller, Clark Gable, Judy Garland, Tom Hanks, Paul Henreid, Betty Hutton, Hope Lange, Angela Lansbury, Cloris Leachman, Fred MacMurray, Mike Ovitz, Gregory Peck, Michelle Pfeiffer, Dennis Quaid, Claude Rains, Rob Reiner, L.A. Mayor Richard Riordan, Meg Ryan, William Saroyan, Jimmy Stewart, Meryl Streep, Shirley Temple

From *City of Quartz* by Mike Davis: *Community in Los Angeles means homogeneity of race, class and, especially, home values. Community designations i.e. the street signs across the city identifying areas as "Canoga Park," "Holmby Hills," "Silverlake" and so on have no legal status. In the last analysis they are merely favors granted by city council members to well-organized neighborhoods or businessmen's groups seeking to have their areas identified.*

*   *   *

It is almost impossible to locate someone who knows where Brentwood begins and ends, as though certainty of boundary would imperil land values. Slightest nuances of undesirability can considerably affect the resale value of property in transient neighborhoods such as Brentwood, where over 80 percent of the population arrived since 1980.

Only a U.S. Post Office map marked with colored pencils inside the Barrington Station yields definitive results. Brentwood, (rather, *90049*) is a squiggly Vermont-shaped rectangle, delineated by Wilshire, Centinella, Montana and 26th on the south, the American Veterans Association grounds and the 405 Freeway and Sepulveda on the east, Mulholland Drive on the north, Sullivan Canyon Fire Road on the west.

Technically, Brentwood also includes the Los Angeles National Cemetery east of the 405—the Arlington Cemetery of the West—as well as parts of Bel Air, though it would be a grueling fight to the death for Bel Aireans to accept this notion.

Brentwood has an ironically mall-like name. (There are no known records of how its name came about; it emerged *ex vacuo* in 1907.) Malls, however, don't exist in Brentwood—not the double-anchor, parking lot for 3,000–style malls of the edge cities. There is, however, a mini-mall at the corner of Barrington and San Vicente that sells Francis Bacon lithographs; on the berm where most other malls might have anti-loitering lighting systems installed sits a line of small Henry Moores.

From Brentwood's inception at the turn of this century, retail was seen as a land value detractor and has persistently been kept at bay. The almost poignant notion of the "country club," however, is as a land value enhancer; the Brentwood Country Club has 500 members.

At Hamburger Hamlet, next to the Henry Moore–sculptured mini-mall, a NASA retiree boasts of having had ten responses to an ad in the local paper asking for "an intelligent, sociologically aware woman."

*   *   *

Social note: at the restaurants, al fresco dining is passé; shade is in; not because of UV's but because one side effect of the new families of antidepressants is photosensitivity. It is not considered indiscreet or even stigmatized to appear in public greased with post–cosmetic surgery Polysporin, nose plasters or wraparound dark glasses.

To further fragment Brentwood would be to break it down into smaller, mallishly named neighborhoods: Westridge, Kenter Canyon, San Vicente Park, Brentwood Heights, Crestwood, Brentwood Park, Westgate, Brentwood Terrace, Mountaingate. Most of these are ruled by homeowners associations who enforce to the best of their ability rules and regulations that will prevent a neighborhood from going "downhill." Much of Brentwood is without sidewalks (drifters!).

Brentwood's main streets are Sunset (an east/west corridor), Bundy (a north/south corridor and Nicole Brown Simpson's street) and the somewhat retail San Vicente, Wilshire, Barrington, running east/west.

MESSAGE BOARD AT THE WESTWARD HO MARKET NEAR THE CORNER OF BARRINGTON AND SAN VICENTE

Effective personal protection. Easy to use. Better than mace or pepper spray.
Cannot be used against you. 310 207-XXXX
Benedict Canyon house for rent. 4-bdrm, hdwd floors, quiet patio, 2-car garage.
$1,800/month
Westec patrol officer seeks guest house for rent.
[Various index cards touting home computer training, home security systems and pizza ovens. A vogue for home pizza ovens seems to have apparently come to an end.]
1976 Porsche 911S Targa. $10,000

One has a hunch that in 1964 the same billboard harbored index cards offering dance lessons, free kittens and piano lessons.

The local newspaper, the *Brentwood News*, a puree of local chitchat fueled by real-estate-driven editorial, follows Brentwood's home sales minutiae with seemingly pornographic fidelity, chronicling monthly the ebb and flow of land capital followed by ads for local properties.

Real estate perhaps is still *the* driving force of conversation in Brentwood. Subdivision maps, and lots resembling cross-cut vacuoles of loofa sponges are a recurring civic visual motif in newspapers, drawn on bar napkins and faxed between neighbors from house to house.

DISPLAY ADVERTISING IN THE BRENTWOOD NEWS

CPAs
law firms
picnic baskets
gem appraisals
cellular phones
local Cartier dealer
Glendale Federal Bank
electronic security systems
Mountain Gate Country Club
Mercedes-specific car repairs
chronic fatigue syndrome counseling
ArmorCoat anti-earthquake window glass
post-earthquake stress counseling seminars
seismically reinforced document storehouses
background investigations and asset searches
tummy- and butt-specific aerobic reduction classes
separation, divorce, custody, visitation, paternity, property division legal specialists

*   *   *

Lower Brentwood, or rather, the lower *part* of Brentwood below San Vicente (referred to by a local youngster as "Nieder Brentwald"), is a mishmash of higher-density rental units, war bride bungalows and Los Angeles generica in the style of Ed Ruscha's mid-1960s paintings.

Tiny Spanish bungalows sit alone; the shielding trees out front died long ago and were never replaced, overexposing the structures to daily solar flare, lowering their land values in the extreme.

The housing density is higher by far in this portion of Brentwood: three-story rental and condo units, most of them toting VACANCY signs, all of them designed in the usual clutter of styles, predominantly DesiLu Moderne, 101 Dalmatians–Mansard, Orange County 1986–Mission and Anaheim-Motel.

Lower Brentwood's plantings, like too many actors at a party, are exotic yet not rare: Waikiki plants—hibiscus, bougainvillea and banana. It is a neighborhood of $900-range renters with nice cars owned by aspiring actors, screenwriters, models and creative types mixed with pensioners. Lower Brentwood's range of reasonably affordable accommodations means that bodyworking men and women can assume night jobs, reserving their days for auditions and the gym.

This is where Brentwood's sexually charged party mix derives its midday and nighttime soap opera ecology.

This Brentwood "underside" is by no means impoverished, yet certainly several cuts below what lies on the other side of San Vicente and above Sunset. It was into this neighborhood that Nicole Brown Simpson landed after her divorce, in a $650,000 condo near the noisy southwest corner of Bundy and Dorothy, on Bundy, a condo that would cost maybe $350,000 were it in most other parts of the city.

One Brentwood resident who grew up in Brentwood Heights (above Sunset; equidistant from Monroe's and Simpson's houses), now in his twenties, calls lower Brentwood a divorcée ghetto. Three of his best friends from high school had parents who divorced, and all three mothers ended up "in the ghetto. Only my own mother [also a divorcée] got to keep the house. She's the exception."

Brentwood, like many West Coast urban districts, acts as a living guide to what might be termed a catalogue of the new temptations:

instant wealth
emotionally disengaged sex
information overload
belief in the ability of ingested substances to alter the aura
of one's flesh or personality architecture
neglect of the maintenance of democracy
willful ignorance of history
body manipulation
willful rejection of reflection
body envy
belief that spectacle is reality
vicarious living through celebrities
rejection of sentiment
unwillingness to assign hierarchy to values

The punchline to this particular cataloguing is that the link between temptation and sin has been severed. Temptation is simply "things one either does or does not do." This leads to one possible question: Is amorality a state of mind that requires hard work to achieve, or is it a state of mind achieved by default? Another question is raised: *Is amorality even up for moral inspection?* Brentwood shows us what people can do . . . if they can.

Brentwood is also technically the 12-step program capital of the planet. The University Synagogue at the corner of Sunset and Saltair every Wednesday between 7:00 and 10:00 P.M. hosts the world's largest weekly Alcoholics Anonymous meeting, with 1,100 attendees.

While held within a synagogue, it is important to remember that AA is non-denominational while at the same time accepting of a higher power.

Driving through Westwood Village en route to Brentwood, amid a Persepolis of dental clean skyscrapers, a friend driving the car proudly proclaims, "See all these buildings? Full of shrinks. Every single one of them. Ain't that great?"

From *The Day of the Locust*:

> They were savage and bitter, especially the middle-aged and the old, and had been made so by boredom and disappointment. . . . Where else should they go but to California, the land of sunshine and oranges? Once they got there, they discovered that sunshine wasn't enough. They get tired of oranges, even of avocado pears and passion fruit. Nothing happens. They don't know what to do with their time. . . . Their boredom becomes more and more terrible. They realize they have been tricked and burn with resentment . . . The sun is a joke. . . . Nothing can ever be violent enough to make taut their slack minds and bodies. They have been cheated and betrayed.

One is reminded in a way of Las Vegans, endlessly pumping their life's dividends into the computer poker units, willfully forgetting their own tired, boring, statistically average personal narratives, narratives so average that they are worthy of self-contempt, in the hope of achieving a random transcendence. Denarrated, like pensioners gambling away their checks somewhere in the nicotine-soaked carpets of Fremont Street, Brentwooders hope to win back their lives, their stories with randomness.

*   *   *

From *TV Guide* (August 6, 1994, issue, on stands August 4, 1994) cover story:

DOES TV NEWS SNUB GOD?

A profile of Peggy Wehmeyer: "Ninety percent of Americans believe in God, why is this woman the only religion reporter on TV?"

Peggy Wehmeyer, ABC's hot new religion reporter, starts her day with an hour of exercise, meditation and prayer. "My spirituality has to do with how I live my life," says the buoyant blonde hired last January by Peter Jennings for World News Tonight's *"American Agenda" segment. "I'm definitely on a spiritual journey, but my church is not the focal point."*

There is a blurring of denominations and attitudes in Brentwood. At one point in the late 1980s and early 1990s, Christians and Jews in Brentwood, Santa Monica and nearby Mar Vista shared the same Mar Vista church building. The *L.A. Times* reports: *"the indoor crosses are covered up for the Jewish services and the Torah scrolls required for the weekly reading from the Hebrew Scriptures are stored in an ark on wheels."*

A sense of spiritual communality based on a ZIP code is truly an act of faith, and so perhaps a broader definition of faith is called for here. Let *faith* represent the location in which we, as citizens, locate our faith for a better tomorrow—what one *believes in* as opposed to what one merely wants to *get*.

Brentwoodians basically agree on good infrastructure, good land values, high security, goodwill toward neighbors (up to a point, after which social atomization sets in), the rewards of rational behavior and increasingly, the payoff of random jackpots.

*　　*　　*

Henry Gris/FPG

Brentwood's mood is *noir*, that particularly Los Angeles phenomenon. One definition of *noir* (again, from Mike Davis's *City of Quartz*) is of "the moral phenomenology of the depraved or ruined middle classes." Is it possible to see Brentwood as the municipal embodiment of the crisis of secularism?

HOUSE OF WORSHIP TALLY

Synagogues	4
Christian	2
Christian Science	2

On Sunday mornings at Bel Air Presbyterian on Mulholland Drive, the other side of the street from Brentwood's northern edge: white-gloved, tan-shirted, brown-pantsed LAPD officers guiding the crush of traffic in and around the church. Infrastructure meets the transcendental.

Driving down San Vicente, past five kilometers of coral trees (*erythrina caffra*) planted in the center median, one realizes that *this* is the land of the fatted calf, the secular nirvana, the citizens of whom Bennie and the Jets invoked to "*plug into the faithless.*"

Psychology Today (July/August 1994) cover story:

ON THE ROAD TO HAPPINESS: WHAT IT IS, WHO HAS IT, AND HOW TO GET THERE

Reports Ed Diener, Ph.D., U. of Illinois, "Put simply, frequent positive experiences are both necessary and sufficient to produce the state we call happiness, whereas *random* [my italics] intense experiences are not."

John Reich, Ph.D., Arizona State U. says, "Winning a lottery may make you happy for a short while, but a *random* [my italics] event, occurring without input, will not create long-term happiness."

Both doctors demonize randomness, in flagrant defiance of the lifestyle of a good many of Brentwood's rental class, comprised in good part of a never-ending flow of actors who spend their hours gigolo-ing, dealing, auditioning whatever all in order to garner the magic scratch-'n'-win lottery ticket of media fame.

Later on, reference is made to Vice President Al Gore's statement that "the accumulation of material goods is at an all-time high, but so is the number of people who feel emptiness in their lives."

Brentwood is a place that has never thought of itself as even existing. That is part of its charm, its attraction. Brentwood has no published written history as do neighboring Malibu, Pacific Palisades, Westwood (the municipal egg containing the yolk of UCLA) or Bel Air or Beverly Hills.

Its entire paper archives fit snugly inside a cardboard Kinko's box inside a librarian's Buick Le Sabre trunk.

From *We Will Always Live in Beverly Hills* by Ned Wynn (Penguin).

> He looked at me and made a face. "Is your dad Van Johnson or not?" he demanded.
>
> "He's my stepfather," I said. "Keenan Wynn's my father." I waited for the awe, the *homage*.
>
> "Never heard of that guy. My sister's big on movie stars, but I don't care about them one *iota*. They're all phonies, anyway, not real people."
>
> I felt my skin prickle.
>
> "They are *so* real," I said.
>
> "*Sure* they are," he said. I swallowed and my eyes started to sting.
>
> "My dad is real," I choked. "He lives in Brentwood."

*   *   *

The Economist (August 6, 1994, on stands, August 4, 1994) cover story:

DOES IT MATTER WHERE YOU ARE?

To express an interest in Brentwood is to try to express interest in an entity unsure if it even possesses any memory.

Most people's first reaction is, "But there *is* no history."

This is followed by "Really?" followed by a suspicious "*How come?* How can you care about a place that doesn't even *exist*?"

It could be that the citizens collectively are involved either in self-deprecation or amnesia. "*You mean this counts as a place?*" or "*How vulgar to talk about one-self.*"

Brentwood has never dreamed of having a profile and possesses a concomitant need to disassociate itself from the ever-encroaching Los Angeles on the east. Citizens migrated to Brentwood for the express luxury of inhabiting a place where there is no "here." Brentwood, unlike higher-profile sister suburbs Bel Air, Westwood and Beverly Hills, has willfully engineered a transparent profile. It is as though to live in Brentwood, one signs a covenant of invisibility. The suburb's existence is a consensual denial of civic randomness and chaos.

If people here are annoyed with O. J. Simpson, possible double murder aside, it is only because he broke the covenant of invisibility. The corner of Rockingham and Ashford is going to be a tourist attraction for the next one hundred years, like it or not. Will this affect land values? Yes. But in which way, who is to know? Michelle Pfeiffer, although she lives below Sunset, has already chosen to move away to avoid the hubbub.

356 Rockingham will become a tourist destination the way the Menendez house in Beverly Hills never will. (Ironic footnote: Eric Menendez and Simpson share adjacent jail cells. To O.J.'s noisy proclamations of innocence, Menendez allegedly retorts, "Save it for someone who *cares*, O.J.")

*   *   *

Seven weeks previously, on June 13, 1994, arrived the shocking eruption of infrastructure's trappings into an until-then Edenic locale: helicopters, news vans, uncontrolled crowds, images of the freeway system monopolized by a single car, megaphones, police cars, satellite dishes, everything that had been wished away and paid extravagantly to avoid had exploded over them like a 1950s Bikini Island test.

Infrastructure: this is a key:

Imagine viewing North America as *terra virginea* almost utterly uninhabited as it was four centuries ago. A continent of shelves and ridges and deltas and arroyos and plains. An unlikely place for a city would be Los Angeles, located almost nowhere, with *nothing*.

One must never overlook the fact that Los Angeles is an entirely *manufactured* city, assembled, piece by piece, largely during the early- to mid-twentieth-century Fordist heyday. Los Angeles without sci-fi-caliber infrastructure is not only unimaginable but impossible.

Freeways, their signage, aqueducts, graveyards, electrical grids and telephone poles—the sexy enormity of these infrastructural intrusions are often a visitor's largest takeaway memory of the place. How many grids overlap other grids overlap grids? Aqueducts, power lines, freeways, signage . . .

And as the city's economy goes post-industrial, its psychic ecology contorts correspondingly.

The dream of American Arcadian livability for Brentwood was actually generated by a Canadian from New Brunswick, Robert C. Gillis, who led a group that in 1904 purchased what is now Brentwood and much of Santa Monica and Pacific Palisades. It was Gillis who ensured tree-lined boulevards and rigid deed restrictions to maintain the area's livability in an era when restrictions were few. Automobile travel was eagerly fostered with oiled roads, which were then paved as soon as possible.

Brentwood's infrastructure is seamless. Its invisibility and fail-proofness all add to the utopian claim of the place.

In Brentwood, infrastructure is present precisely through its *lack* of presence. A strong component of Brentwood's identity is that the area acts as a temporary respite from the infrastructural omnipresence of Los Angeles. Brentwood was designed to emulate the country, seen as a retreat from a too-rapidly growing city, with ample setbacks of houses and "massive plantings of trees" ensuring relief.

Entering Brentwood is like reading a book where the capitalization periods and commas suddenly vanish

It is a suburb in denial of technology, yet all-demanding in its need for technology to provide illusions generated by denial.

"A butterfly should be able to fly through any properly kept tree," is the local axiom.

Trees are a huge issue in this community.

Trees separate the rich from the poor and sustain a bucolic illusion, which in turn sustains land values. Most important, *trees mask the power poles, transformer boxes and all other infrastructural blights.*

Most are maintained with due precision: Bower Wattle, Peppermint Tree, Bunya-Bunya, Avocado, Carrot Wood, California Pepper, Loquat, Weeping Chinese Banyan, Jacaranda, New Zealand Tea Tree, Olive, Victorian Box and Lemonade Berry. Cumulatively they add up to one meaning: *Heaven is manufacturable.*

But trees, like the citizens of Brentwood, are facing the problems of Los Angeles "the encroacher." Trees regularly die due to heavy construction, grade changes, overwatering, strangling ivy, smog, drought. There are limits to how much change can be absorbed.

And not just the trees, but the plants! Brentwood nurtures an almost infinite array of plantings: grassy Low bullrush, chive, Shamrock, spinach-like Acanthus,

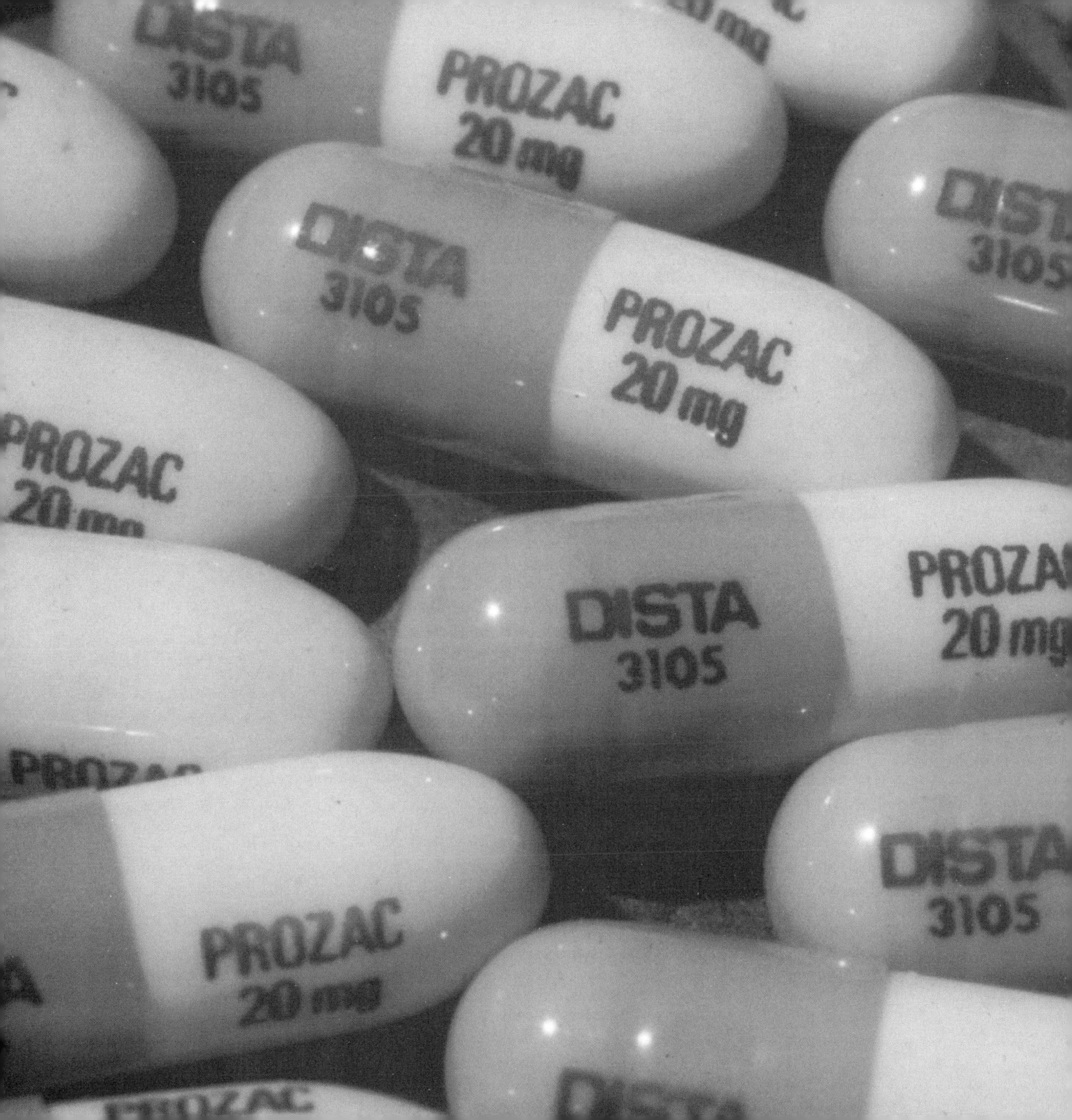
DISTA
3105
PROZAC
20 mg
DISTA
3105
PROZAC
20 mg
PROZAC
DISTA
3105
PROZAC
20 mg
DISTA
3105

succulent Stonecrop and Houseleek, feathery Gru-gru palms, flowered Choreopsis and the omni-present Delft-blue Lily-of-the-Nile such as those that lined Nicole Brown Simpson's condominium walkway, technically called *aga-panthus*, at their height in July and August.

* * *

There is a growing notion in academic circles and perceived viscerally in the chakras of Brentwoodians that cities—Shanghai; Mexico; Lagos; Los Angeles—can simply grow for*ever,* that there are no real limits yet found as to how many people may agglomerate in one place. As Brentwood is increasingly encircled, will it remain an island or will it be strangled?

* * *

Infrastructure highlight: Monday nights, garbage night, when tight clusters of Wedgwood blue and gunmetal gray Rubbermaid "Bruiser" 32-gallon wheeled refuse containers huddle at driveway feet. Some households have up to 18 containers at a time. There are also City of Los Angeles recycling containers: red for metal; yellow for glass.

INFRASTRUCTURAL HIGHLIGHTS OF BRENTWOOD AND BRENTWOOD PARK (NEIGHBORHOOD OF O. J. SIMPSON)

1907	Ads in the *Los Angeles Times* extol Brentwood's virtues.
1922	Brentwood's lands are only one-quarter sold; the firm of Shipley, Harrell and Trapp takes over.
1942	Brentwood Park's homeowners association formed in response to the threat of subdivision and lowering land values.
1963	Lot subdivisions are limited to 20,000 square feet.
1970	Caesar Romero, actor, and June Lockhart, actress, shear apart a ribbon, inaugurating the new post office at 137 Barrington Avenue. Romero wears his trademark cravat and

a carnation in his vest; Lockhart dons a pre-wedge/post-pixie hairdo and wears an A-line linen dress.

1975	There is a momentary burst of fear when San Vicente Boulevard is possibly to be renamed a highway.
1977	Further panic when plans for a freeway along Sunset, straight through the center of Brentwood, are proposed. Plan eventually killed by coalition of homeowners associations and environmental groups.
1978	A vote among Brentwood Park Homeowners Association members allows, by a narrow margin, a limit of two on-location film shoots per residence per year.
1980	Mace instruction classes are formed.
1984	A mailing is sent out on how to conceal trash cans.
1985	Underground wiring is left as a block-by-block decision.
1990	A general survey is held regarding "undergrounding" of utility wires.
1991	Water rationing.
1991	Leaf blower noise limited to 65 decibels.
1993	Magnetic fields in nearby Kenter Canyon are halved by the Department of Water and Power owing to possible leukemia health risk.

All of this is history, but then the past is something Brentwood seems somewhat indifferent to, even with the near one-billion-dollar J. Paul Getty Center, an elegant monolith atop a hill halfway between Sunset Boulevard and Mulholland Drive west of the 405.

Designed by Richard Meier, scheduled for a 1997 opening and surfaced with travertine, the center is the largest project in cost and dimension currently under way in the United States, and possibly, after the cancellation of the Texan Waxahachie supercollider, the most complex.

But the Getty is not yet a part of the lives of Brentwoodians and maybe never will be. It does not collect twentieth-century art, and it is too remote from the inhabited suburbs to lend any warmth of presence.

The physical presence of the Getty atop its hill acts as a stunning metaphor for the weight of history placed in a location that is silently and willfully antagonistic toward recognizing history's flow.

*   *   *

Most Brentwood residential structures were built between 1950 and 1979. Fewer than 10 percent have been built since then. Most of the houses built in the neighborhood's Brentwood Hills subdivision were built in the 1960s and 1970s by Art Linkletter.

A drive in any portion of Brentwood reveals a chocolate box of architectural styles:

MGM-Colonial-Scandalbox
San-Diego-Public-School-System-post-and-beam
Marcus-Welby-Sonorous-Tudor (the Simpson house)
1941-white-stucco-Pearl-Harbor's-just-been-bombed-Cocktail, Darling?
Doris-Day's-in-the-house-holding-a-lobster-claw-and-dish-of-melted-butter-
Cape Cod
The-future-*Whoosh!*-Apollo-17
Kim-Novak's-Love-Nest-Ranchero

From *We Will Always Live in Beverly Hills* by Ned Wynn (about the house of his stepfather, Van Johnson).

The house itself was a sleek Deco/Moderne cube that my friend Jackie
Hathaway called Uncle Scrooge's money bin.

*   *   *

On September 14, 1993, the Los Angeles City Council passed the Hillside Ordinance by an 11 to 2 vote preventing the "mansionization" or the creation of what is known in other cities as "monster houses" by land developers who, throughout the 1980s, would tear down smaller houses, carefully examine local building codes and then build the largest possible structure legally allowed on the same property. The not-often-pleasing-to-neighbors result was then flipped for a fat profit.

One particularly popular style for these new "monster houses" is one that might be called "San-Fernando-Valley-mini-mall": a fevered dream of the Mediterranean, a house where Barbie might live, hugely overpedimented, grossly and arrogantly disproportionate to all surrounding structures, cake-frosted with stucco and lacking only a Plexiglas sign saying *Ralphs* or *Tower Records* or *Glossy Nails*.

Monsters.

In the 1960s, monsters were googly-eyed, Rat Fink, Revell model chummy things, anonymously designed folkloric terror, and lovable at the core: Incredible Edibles; Wacky Packs; Herman Munster. But what is our vision of monsters *now*? There no longer seems to be friendliness attached to them; they are now merely out to kill (just visit any video rental shop), either that or they're out to—*shiver*—devalue our neighborhoods.

If the monsters we create as a culture reflect our deepest terrors temporarily focused into one entity like Frankenstein, killer robots, pod people, then with the monster house, Brentwood has spawned monsters of a new toughness, durability and sublimity.

The Hillside Ordinance against monster houses might then be likened to "stuffed monster," something given to children to help them objectify and reduce their fears. By giving children beasts small enough to manipulate, it makes them feel as though they are really in charge.

*   *   *

Sample ad from the real estate section of the *Brentwood News:*

"AUTHENTIC HACIENDA"

    This 3-bedroom, 3-bath gated estate in Brentwood is being offered through Douglas Properties for $1,025,000.

    Offering tremendous privacy, this authentic hacienda features an inviting courtyard, large family room, formal dining room, breakfast area, and a separate guest house or staff quarters plus cabana.

    Charming details include wood beam ceilings, tile floors and stained-glass windows. The home is suffused with natural light through skylights. Dream-like gardens lead to a pool and spa and cabana. The setting affords privacy just minutes from the heart of Brentwood.

The "ranch-style house" was literally invented in Brentwood, in Sullivan Canyon, by Clifford May. In a *New York Times* interview he pronounced, *"The ranch house was everything a California house should be. It had cross-ventilation, the floor was level with the ground and with the courtyard and with the exterior corridor. It was about sunshine and gracious living."*

May tried to blur the definition of the inside and the outside. Prominent fireplaces with wood and stone are a dominant theme. Tiling inside and outside his houses minimize indoor/outdoor distinctions; all rooms look outward; sliding glass doors and skylights connect the two realms.

May's was an aesthetic idealized and mass-produced in post-WWII booms, deeply winding its way into the popular consciousness of successive generations

raised in subdivisions and multiple *Bewitched* reruns. May is one of the secret, dominant forces of why most Americans quickly and readily are able to embrace "California."

AFTERNOON

Marilyn Monroe was entombed in Westwood, just across the 405 Freeway from Brentwood, at Westwood Memorial Cemetery, 1218 Glendon Avenue, one block south of Wilshire Boulevard's Golden Mile directly behind the 25-story Wells Fargo Tower, almost 32 years ago. Truman Capote, for whatever the coincidence is worth, is entombed perhaps 250 feet away in the same structure.

The cemetery, smaller than half a baseball field, is almost empty today, the anniversary of her death. The smooth walls lining its perimeter, like those of the Getty, are built of beige travertine and provide an echo that reminds one of what silence is supposed to be, a difficult task amid the urban roar. The banking tower's ventilation plant, combined with the thrum of the nearby San Diego Freeway's rush hour and the roar of traffic and LAPD helicopters makes for a somewhat less than Arcadian environment.

Monroe's tomb inserted into the walls of the "Corridor of Memories," much of which was not built at the time of death, is at stomach height behind two feet of concrete, and is kitty-corner from the Memorial Park's main office, a Swiss-chalet-Trader-Vic's-Bank-of-America A-frame hybrid.

On August 4, 1994, Monroe's is the cemetery's only crypt whose marble surface is no longer creamy white. Years of visitors' rubbing hands have smudged it gray with body oils. The brass of her plaque (MARILYN MONROE 1926–1962) is the only plaque among all neighboring plaques that has been polished clean by thousands of hands talismanically glossing its raised letters over the years, like the front door of a Milanese church. It is the most visited grave in Los Angeles.

Today the cistern in front contains a dozen red roses. At its feet lie a bouquet of champagne pink roses and a white basket full of white freesia.

*   *   *

Around 5:00 P.M., a Japanese woman, about 22, with a blotchy complexion and a short, blunt haircut and wearing a sailor-style suit stands gawkishly alone in front of Monroe's crypt.

Awkwardly, she reaches out and pats its cool stone and then stands back. Even more cautiously, she leans forward and kisses the stone's top left corner, leaving behind a small, round, bubble-gum pink lipstick kiss.

She runs away, covering her mouth with her right hand.

After her autopsy, Monroe's hair was soaked in formaldehyde and unstyleable. A wig was borrowed permanently from Fox. Her fair skin, blue from cyanosis, required extraordinary amounts of makeup to re-whiten. She was buried in a lime green Pucci dress with a lime green scarf around her neck.

GREEN REMAINS A DOMINANT BRENTWOOD COLOR:

eucalyptus
tennis court
road signage
citrus
dying lawn (khaki)
thriving lawn (bluegrass)
pear
fig
Jaguar
rubber tree
military green postboxes
Jeep Cherokee

On the radio it is announced that QVC-TV auctioned studio photos taken by Bert Stern six weeks before Monroe's death, her last studio photo session. Home shoppers were able to purchase photos that Monroe had herself desecrated along with that same photo, "de-desecrated" via computer. Top price obtained: $7,900.

Back in Brentwood, and just outsde the Union 76 station at the corner of Bundy and San Vicente, a donation of a dollar, say, purchases you a photocopied sheet of "Poems for Nicole Simpson" by a local street entrepreneur wearing a felt-tip-pen-on-cardboard sign saying: MORE POEMS ABOUT NICOLE SIMPSON. Business is brisk. Locals say, "At least he's offering something original and new."

On San Vicente Boulevard, dark rumors float about Brentwood's no-fat cafes, phone machines and the brightly lit aisles of the Vicente Market—rumors too dark, too dreadful to mention, for to speak the word is to give life, and who will spawn this monster?

Perhaps these rumors are true. Perhaps time will tell. Perhaps it will all be forgotten.

Meanwhile, to hinder the "lookie-loo's," thru-traffic is blocked on both sides of Dorothy. An LAPD officer beside his motorcycle keeps traffic flowing.

The front of the alleyway in which the bodies of Nicole Brown Simpson and Ronald Lyle Goldman were found has been screened off by a dozen or so dwarf maples still inside their black PVC nursery tubs. It is further hidden by previous plantings of Australian tree ferns and Nile lilies behind a new enclosure of green-plasticated chain-link fence that separates the walkway from the sidewalk (*this* part of Brentwood has sidewalks).

Signs put up by agitated neighbors saying "GET A LIFE" and "GO HOME THERE IS NOTHING 2 SEE" have been taken down. By August 4, late afternoon traffic no longer concertinas to a grind the way it did in the initial sensationalist frenzy of a few weeks ago. But it still slows down.

There are a few joggers and dog walkers—Brentwood's only two species of residential pedestrian—and all are wearing Walkmans.

It was a dogwalker who first found the murdered bodies.

GO HOME
THERE IS
NOTHING 2 SEE

LATE AFTERNOON

It is now approaching sunset time. We think back to August 4, 1962: This is the night, 32 years ago, when Marilyn Monroe tried to decide, "Will I or won't I take the pills?" (or perhaps others speaking the words, "How will *we* administer the poison?").

Brentwood dreaming, dreaming whether or not to live or die.

The cul-de-sac behind her old house at 12305 Fifth Helena, but a bone's throw from the old house of Raymond Chandler, is silent. There are desiccated lemons strewn on gravel, bird of paradise clippings in the trash bin, a Washingtonia palm with a frazzled, untrimmed skirt, gardeners' pickup trucks, an air-conditioning company van and day lilies.

Around 7:00 P.M., while walking amid the streets of Brentwood from the old Monroe neighborhood up to Rockingham, one observes the arcana of upper-middle-class Californiana: skateboard stickers on top of the Stop signs; picket fences; plentiful bottle-brush trees in bloom; the smell of lilies and roses; random pockets of deep silence; security cameras silently rotating as they scan pedestrians *en passant*; brick and mortar mounds bound for the landfill; domestic help leaving late for the day; mourning doves cooing on the telephone lines.

The air is cleaner now than it would have been in 1962. There are more cars in 1994, but they pollute less than when pre-unleaded tanks spewed blue smoke into the sky like lawnmowers. But there is undeniably more *noise*: crickets; drowsy songbirds; the whistling wings of startled, escaping doves who have been enjoying the end-of-day heat on the asphalt; the cawing of crows in the cedar deodorus; the drone of pool filters—these are the eternal sounds. But the traffic on Sunset a third of a mile up the hill would certainly not have been so loud in 1962 as it is tonight, nor would there have been the helicopters—LAPD copters, radio trafficopters and the tabloid and TV copters zooming in above Rockingham, even still, weeks later.

*   *   *

To appear "well maintained" in Brentwood is, of course, a beyond-discussion ultradesirable West Coast pursuit: firm, symmetrical blemish-free bodies. As the London *Sunday Times*'s *Culture* magazine stated, California represents the "democratization of beauty."

Yet rarely, if ever, is the question asked of the body-obsessed, *"Just what is it you expect to get from your body? What is it you want your body to do for you that it isn't doing for you right now?"*

Nicole Brown Simpson was a body fanatic, 5'8", 125 lbs.; she was homecoming queen in Dana Point, California; she jogged three miles a day; she ate only low/no-fat food and attended gyms regularly.

Like Monroe, Nicole Brown Simpson was intensely aware of her power over men, and well aware of her ability to pick and choose partners as she pleased. Her white Ferrari, won in her October 1992 divorce case with Simpson, had vanity plates reading L84AD8 ("Late for a date"). Those spurned by Brown Simpson's attentions grudgingly admit to her almost otherworldly desirability and bear her no ill will. "She had that *well-maintained look*," is one comment.

Gyms, in general, are notorious cash points for steroids and cocaine. It is rare to encounter a gym rat—male or female—without quickly finding somebody with evident emotional difficulties.

From *Makeover* magazine, a new publication of *People*, released the first week of August:

BRUNETTE TO BLONDE

A 2½-page spread entitled: Using Marilyn Monroe as the "ultimate blonde" transformation.

Winners include Madonna, Bette Midler, Iman, Hillary Rodham Clinton and Roseanne Arnold.

Losers include Julia Roberts, Angelica Huston, Demi Moore, Geena Davis,

Delta Burke and, surprisingly, Loni Anderson, whose hair was once described by Bill Griffiths' cartoon character, Zippy the Pinhead, to "mounds of hardened Cool-Whip."

Hello! magazine (UK), August 2, 1994, issue:

CHILD OF DARKNESS, KATY GREEN: THE POIGNANT STORY OF THE TEN-YEAR-OLD BORN TO LIVE IN A TWILIGHT WORLD

Katy Green of Saltney, England, suffers from congenital erythropoietic por-phyria (CEP), a condition in which the faintest light, even the moon, television, car headlights, causes her skin to blister, fever, headaches.

She can only enter the outer world completely hidden, masked and protected. Too many flashbulbs could conceivably, if not kill her, then injure her, cripple her.

After a while one becomes used to the Brentwood notion of the superior body and superior, invisible infrastructure—as well as a subtly implicit neighborhood atti-tude that any hierarchy of ideas is, if not corny, then perhaps antique.

After a certain amount of exposure to the neighborhood, tears elicit only fear, not sympathy . . . Are you . . . *unglued?* Stop crying. After a while, people from *elsewhere* seem naïve and unarmored. One drives through Pennsylvania, for example, and sees freeway overpasses obviously not up to any State of California seismic code and wonders, *"What's going through their minds—don't they* know*?"*

* * *

From *Dino,* a biography of Dean Martin by Nick Tosches:

> Nineteen-fucking-eighty. He had outlived Crosby. He outlived Elvis. He had outlived Terry's Wonder Dogs. He would outlive them all. He had discovered the secret of happiness.
>
> "How's it going?" someone asked him at the Riviera Country Club one day.

"Beautiful," he said. "It's great. I wake up every morning. Massive bowel movement. The Mexican maid makes me some breakfast. Down to the club here. At least nine holes. A nice lunch. Go home, sit by the TV. The Mexican maid makes me a nice dinner. A few drinks. Go to bed. Wake up the next morning. Another massive bowel movement. Beautiful. This is my life."

Ten years later, Martin is a walking corpse, drinking himself into the grave nightly at Dan Tana's on Santa Monica Boulevard in West Hollywood. For Martin, all narrative rationales have imploded. What's the point?

From the menu of Gratis! Fat Free Cuisine on San Vicente Boulevard:

Bowl of Black Bean Soup	$2.95
(garnished with sour cream unless otherwise requested)	
Herbed Ricotta Raviolis with Marinara Sauce	$7.95
Side of Mashed Potatoes & Caramelized Onion Gravy	$1.75
Barbecued Zucchini Pizza	$6.95
Raspberry Roulade	$2.75

It has been said that as animals, one factor that sets us apart from all other animals is that our lives need to be stories, narratives, and that when our stories vanish, that is when we feel lost, dangerous, out of control and susceptible to the forces of randomness. It is the process whereby one loses one's life story: "denarration."

Denarration is the technical way of saying, "not having a life."

"Scott doesn't have a life"; "Amber is denarrated."

Up until recently, no matter where or when one was born on earth, one's culture provided one with all components essential for the forging of identity. These components included: religion, family, ideology, class strata, a geography, politics and a sense of living within a historic continuum.

Suddenly, around ten years ago, with the deluge of electronic and information media into our lives, these stencils within which we trace our lives began to vanish, almost overnight, particularly on the West Coast. It became possible to be alive yet have no religion, no family connections, no ideology, no sense of class location, no politics and no sense of history. Denarrated.

In a low-information environment, pre-TV, etc., relationships were the only form of entertainment available. Now we have methods of information linkage and control ranging from phone answering machines to the Internet that mediate relationships to the extent that corporeal interaction is now beside the point. As a result, the internal dialogue has been accelerated to whole new planes as regularized daily contact has become an obsolete indulgence.

The West Coast continues to be a laboratory of denarration. In a very odd sense, the vacuum of nothingness forces the individual either to daily reinvent himself or herself or perish. Therefore it should come as no surprise that, sunny weather aside, Hollywood and the dream-creation apparatus of the twentieth century should locate itself in a planetary locale of relative blackness.

Q: Who are you this week? This year?

Denarration seems to be the inevitable end-product of information supersaturation, and because it appears to be an inevitable condition, like a hurricane off the Florida coast, it is not on the moral spectrum.

Smugly non-denarrated locales such as Europe, now swamped by media technology taken for granted for decades in North America, now suddenly look to North America for clues or answers as to how to cope with the sensation of personal storylessness. The cautionary tales of Brentwood, where total denarration

Richard Mackson/FPG

has been in full swing since the early 1960s (Marilyn) offer examples, and possibly advice.

Excerpt from a note written by Simpson prior to his Sand Diego Freeway "chase": *"Please think of the real O.J. and not this lost person."*

Simpson once told *Sports Illustrated* about fame: *"You realize if you're living an image, you're just not living."*

One wonders if sentimentalizing the mid-twentieth-century notion of life seems at worst unproductive. Buying into an untenable 1950s narrative of what "life" is supposed to be can only lead to useless and uncreative expenditures of energy. How are we to know that people with "no lives" aren't really on the new frontier of human sentience and perception?

The July 2, 1994, issue of Britain's celebrity-glorifying glossy magazine *Hello!* might well be considered the "All-Brentwood-Post-Fame" issue.
    Hello!, famous for the consistently unthreatening stance it takes on the subjects it portrays with multiple, always-flattering color photos ("At Home with Mr. Satan: Lucifer pats his furry pal Cerberus and contemplates life without love: *'I'm looking for a full-time relationship, but it's hard when so many people rely on you.'* Flames add a country touch to the spacious underground home of Mr. Satan, referred to as 'Bub' by his many friends"). Fergie happily does *Hello!* spreads as do many otherwise media-skittish entities.
    Pages 42 and 43: The Princess of Wales, in a now-rare public appearance, refusing to look into the camera lens.
    Pages 44 and 45: Synopsis of the O. J. Simpson story.
    Pages 50 to 57 (cover story): Ex–Mrs. Rod Stewart/George Hamilton, Alana Stewart warmly discusses breast implant–removal trauma and gives readers many glimpses into her stylish Brentwood home. Included are photos of Stewart with her two children by Stewart, Kimberly and Sean, as well as photos taken with her

Archive Photos

ex-heroin-addict son, Ashley, with a recently broken arm and a facial expression that can be best described as sullen.

Caption: *It was a shock for Alana to learn that her tall and broody son, Ashley, 19 (above), was in intensive care for the second time in a year and a half. Now she's happy to have him back at home and help him recuperate, only ten months after he flew the coop for a headline wedding and whirlwind marriage to Shannen Doherty.*

Within the limits of her biology and intellect, Monroe went as far as it is possible for a human to travel into the hyperspace of fame. After this occurred, sex, high culture, temptations and the sating of earthly desires had lost all attractive charms for her. She had realized the limits of how far the body can take one.

The story of Monroe's life had been stripped away. She had been denarrated and there seemed no other possible narrative arc to her life. No stencil. Marriage? Who would she have married—the president? A career? Been there; done that.

In the end it seemed she was trying too hard to put a pleasant facade onto— nothingness. Her body had become a liability. She had become post-famous. She was first; maybe JFK was second; Elvis was third.

Monroe, empty child of Los Angeles, blank screen, according to Norman Mailer, "free of history." One local guidebook lists 23 separate addresses within Los Angeles where Monroe had lived since her birth.

Monroe, not an accumulator by nature, lived in a blazing white, L-shaped red-tiled Spanish-style house furnished casually with junky, funky Mexicana furniture. It contains chunky pine tables, chairs and benches; serape blankets; "Hacienda" '50s motel-type lamps, a small hi-fi in a suitcase with a folding chair next to it stacked with 33⅓ records; a tri-level glass bar; a display wall surfaced in knotty pine. The feeling is anonymous and hotel-like, places where Monroe had lived much of her life.

Her bedroom is a disaster. Teenagers have been grounded for less. Purses and bags heaped up on the floor against a wall. Papers, scripts, pill bottles everywhere.

In the end, the police tried to locate a family member of Monroe, but the only person they could locate was her mother, institutionalized and incompetent. Ex-husband DiMaggio was entrusted with providing a narrative thread to the rituals of entombment.

In the event of no narrative at all, fantastic narratives have forever zoomed in to fill the vacuum.

In Brentwood one sees a certain blankness in the eyes, and if not a blankness, then a *wanting*, as though some form of information has been deleted, personal history and narrative cashed in like frequent flyer points on vacations that failed to amuse within a frighteningly short period of time.

Brentwood is a region of Los Angeles that speaks eloquently of the amorality of cash in its inability by itself to act as a narrative stencil to life. Money is an invention just as much as is a spoon or a plate, and as such is neither moral nor immoral, it is simply an invention like the toaster or the zero. This is always a shock to learn, for Brentwood's first or second generation of upwardly mobile, brood-spawning wealth. What seems to leave its inhabitants almost naïvely stunned is the emptiness of the money once it arrives; its inherent disconnection to morality.

Neither fame nor money add storyline to one's life. This is, since biblical times, the irony of human pursuit and a torpid punchline enacted daily amid Brentwood's salons, cafes and spotlessly clean, freshly beflowered households.

If life is a car traveling down the road at 55 mph, money and fame will change the color of the car, but it won't change the speed or its direction. It is interesting to note that most entertainment whiz kids buy and sell the red Ferrari within a year, almost immediately converting to Audis and Lexuses, and staying there ever thereafter.

There is a sadness. When asked what they want nowadays, young people, with alarming frequency, ask for fame or money, wishing nonlinearity and denarration upon themselves.

*   *   *

Brentwood is a suburb of indeterminate verdicts and unclear death. Murders aren't solved here. Monroe; Brown Simpson; the Menendez brothers in nearby Beverly Hills—their investigations simply drag on until amnesia sedates any enthusiasm for a full solution.

From *The Brentwood News* (August 1994):

SIMPSON'S VOCAL COACH NOTES TONE

Morton Cooper, Ph.D., whom O. J. Simpson began consulting in September of 1983 begins, *"How do you plead? O. J. Simpson answered in a firm, full voice: 'Absolutely, one hundred percent not guilty.' This was the voice I had known, outgoing and resonant."* Cooper continues to note that Simpson had been repeatedly "benched" by sore throats and vocal polyps. *"He was becoming a vocal has-been. Worse, his style of speech was vocal suicide. Constant misuse could wipe out his voice altogether. What is vocal suicide? It is the incorrect use of the voice."*

Cooper continues to tell of how he rescued O.J. from vocal suicide, and how: *"If and when O. J. Simpson testifies, he may very well be the most listened-to man on the planet. Will his voice get him heard, liked and listened to, as it has in the past?"*

There exists the notion of "Post Fame." Post Fame is about the intersection of human biology with information overload; it is about the erasure of privacy in the personal and media realm; it is (pointedly but not measurably) about the *limits* of fame itself.

Post Fame is when fame becomes a liability to its possessor, or rather, the deficits begin to frighteningly outweigh any conceivable benefits. It's when having an actual body becomes either a liability or somewhat beside the point. Pornographic.

Physical existence—the fact that a person can actually eat an apple, wonder

Steve Wisbauer

about the weather, defecate or pick flowers in the garden becomes unbelievable; titillating yet somehow . . . boring.

The increased number of outlets for media has had an effect of both trivializing fame and privacy for both the public and the famous. Never has the line between torpor and fascination been so thin.

Unlike the earnest *Photoplay* obsequiousnesses of the 1950s and 1960s where the star did what was required of him or her for their fans, there is no longer linkage or responsibility between the star and the audience in whose imagination he or she rests. The relationship now has become almost predatory; vampiric.

The notion that the media is something "manipulable" is increasingly being viewed as naïve and untenable.

Post Fame points out the diminishing nature of privacy in modern culture, the unwillingness of celebrities to surrender what few shreds they still possess and the anger of the public at not being able to possess those few shreds. Julia Roberts reports in *People* magazine, "My relationship does not fall under the Freedom of Information Act." While one assumes that the famous have unlisted home numbers, other aspects of their lives become unlisted to the point of public outrage. Many stars are simply refusing to hand out any private details. Revelation is no longer an issue of "privacy" but of *dematerialization*—fear of becoming a living ghost.

We have reached a point where the limits of fame seem to have been finally articulated. Inasmuch as we have learned limits of corporate growth: GM circa 1988; IBM circa 1987; we have perhaps also learned the new growth limits of fame: Michael Jackson circa 1993; Madonna circa 1992.

Post Fame's biggest drawbacks for the famed ones themselves, is the manner in which Post Fame strips life of any conceivable narrative, leaving the Famed one to merely bask in a pool of Famedness, with no storyline, no narrative arc and no pictures of possible futures.

The West Coast, with its lack of history, places a daily psychic pressure on its citizens for continual self-reinvention. If one does not change mates, religions, hairdos, bodies, politics or residence periodically, the secret and vaguely pejorative assumption among natives is: *That person really isn't trying.*

The Simpson episode pornographically exposed the full infrastructure of fame-generating technology in all of its scope, beauty and ugliness. It brought to the forefront issues of semi-stories, contrived stories, and meta-stories.

Post Fame asks: *Are we making it more difficult for people to reinvent themselves? Is the price of reinvention worth the effort? Is charisma now simply too dangerous a thing to be had by its possessor?*

On August 1, it was official: Michael Jackson and Lisa Marie Presley (schooled in Brentwood) were, indeed, married.

The next day the *Los Angeles Times* reported (on page B–1, the Metro section, but *above* the fold): *"In an unprecedented merger of pop dynasties, Elvis Presley's daughter confirmed through a publicist that she and Michael Jackson were married about ten weeks ago in a private ceremony outside the United States."*

On the same page (below the fold) it was reported that "feminist" attorney Gloria Allred called on District Attorney Gil Garcetti to ask for the death penalty against Simpson. *"Allred contended at a downtown news conference that if Garcetti declines to seek the maximum penalty of death, it will indicate that he is showing favoritism to a celebrity defendant."*

Allred wore what appeared to be a laminated ultraglamorous color photo of Nicole Brown Simpson, roughly the size of a playing card, attached to the front of her business suit with a small-size black document clip.

Overheard at Mezzaluna: "They've stopped inventing supermodels."

*   *   *

Conventional wisdom in Brentwood is that "O.J. never looked better than he did in court." He receives 3,500 pieces of love mail a week.

People magazine (August 8, 1994):

CASHING IN

"Innocent or guilty, O.J. isn't simply the accused, he's a brand name."

The New York Times Magazine (June 26, 1994):

TALKING ABOUT THE MEDIA CIRCUS

Barbara Ehrenreich: "There's a new standard. It used to be, get the scoop and be first. Now you want to be 14th or 23rd: 'No, I didn't do it until after NBC did it and ABC did it.' You have to be the last one to do these stories and wear the badge of purity."

Jerry Nachman: "When I was editing the *Post,* I'd get calls from colleagues at newspapers, whose names you would instantly recognize, wondering when and if we were going to pop the 'X' story. And I would ask, 'Are you going to try do it first?' And they would say, 'No, we want to go the next day.' There was a race to see who would be first to go second."

SUNSET/EVENING

No matter what anyone says, Monroe *looked* different during the last few months of her life. Pregnancy? Cosmetic surgery? Depression? During some of the final photos of Monroe taken near the end of her life, her skull began to show through more clearly. She began to resemble someone other than the self that had been manufactured, an actual person.

Her body, her "franchise," was on the brink of erosion. Imagine if McDonald's restaurants suddenly all began to crumble and stink and became sex hangouts; urine-stenched vines growing up the cracked vinyl signage, interiors looted and smeared with feces, graffiti. Entropy is not permitted in the realm of fame.

The notion of body-as-franchise raises a question, the question that perhaps other means of developing idea franchises are going to have to be created other than personality-centered structures. *Perhaps charisma has become too deadly for those who are seduced by its charms, or too deadly for the charismatic him or her self.*

People magazine (June 13, 1994) cover story:

Diana's Daring New Life: Topless bathing? Holistic healing? Aromatherapy? Anything goes as a liberated Diana struggles to find herself.

The cover photo portrays her as a secular Gap goddess, an honorary Brentwoodian: white-toothed, clad in an American football-team jacket, more All-American than effete British. Inside, however, the article then goes on to portray the Princess of Wales as rudderless, filling her days with obsessive, meaningless, body-centric activities.

What makes the case of the Princess of Wales so fascinating is her almost instantaneous and complete rejection of all media and media-mediating technologies, bodyguards and so forth. It is interesting to note that the "search for personal freedom" invariably is a quest sought by the denarrated. It is as though the vision of denarration visited her in a dream, and when she awoke, her life could never be the same.

Her narrative problem is almost Monroe-esque: Who to date? How to date? Where next from here?

While fame in itself adds no narrative dimension to a famous person's life, fame *does* add an element of *chaos* to one's psychic environment that increases its probability of going nonlinear.

Magazines feature endless maps of houses that accompany Brentwood's Post-Fame deaths, blueprints as pornography, the assumption that there exists an empirical blueprint for murder. *"Well, the living room is adjacent to the bedroom." "The alley led to the front door, and her condo was on the right."*

From the *Los Angeles Times* (August 4, 1994):

WHEN HOME SECURITY LOOKS LIKE SIEGE MENTALITY

Two Texans have developed a half-inch thick siding, Safe Shield, that for roughly $4,000 *"will cover the inside of your doors, roof and garage, and for additional protection, sliding panels that cover the windows at night."*

The notion of corporeal security is one of Brentwood's most seductive appeals.

Like left-shoulder inoculation bumps, each Brentwood yard, without exception, brandishes a metal spike-pegged sign indicating the security system(s) with which that property has been vaccinated: Westec, Knight, Brinks, E.E., Southland Home Protectors, Bel Air Home Patrol, and Protection One (1-800 GET HELP) are but a few. Westec is by far the most common.

Multilayered exclusion devices insulate properties from the outer world; a perimetric fence and gate (often monitored by cameras) encloses thick hedgerow vegetation which in turn enclose dogs which in turn surround the house which is tripwired with magnets, beams, contact points, numeric input pads and alarms.

From an April 1994 Brentwood region homeowners association newsletter:
"Follow-home crimes are frequent—use your car mirror and look around! Can you *back* into your driveway? This is a suggestion from the local police."

"Air bags are now being stolen from cars."

"Summer bunco scams: be forewarned about those great bargains for house-painting, driveway refurbishing, etc."

[Phone number for a West L.A. volunteer graffiti removal organization]

"Louvered windows are unsafe and easily removed. By using superglue, you can ensure they won't be removed."

The Veterans Administration Land

On the east side of the 405 is the Los Angeles National Cemetery, still in ZIP code 90049, with 80,000 buried; room for no more.

But this is *not* Arlington. This cemetery is *extremely* undertree-ed, and feels eternally parched, its infinite-seeming rows of graves ever in need of water. Like all cemeteries, it is, of course, a landscape of utter uneventfulness.

Land across the 405 and Sepulveda Boulevard *is* soon enough going to be transferred from the Veterans Administration to the Department of Memorial Affairs to effect a 50 percent expansion of burial capacity. An additional 80 acres at the site's neglected north end will be converted into an arboretum. But this is not a decision that happened easily or lightly.

As one drives from the Los Angeles National Cemetery along Wilshire and underneath the 405, one loops right and is back in Brentwood again turning again right, into the Los Angeles Veterans Administration property: 546 acres between Sunset and Wilshire housing several score of oddly outdated, underfunded-looking Sad Sack–era structures, the only modern building of which, the 17-story that houses 25 agencies, exudes a bizarre aura of time-travel experimentation gone wrong.

This is not 90049; it is 90073.

In the mid-1980s, the Reagan administration declared 109 acres at the north end of the property as surplus, sending ballistic a collection of local interest groups including the American Legion, AMVETS and, not insignificantly, the Brentwood and Westwood homeowners groups, who in turn formed the Veterans Park Preserve and effectively killed the land-sale deal, instead initiating a program to enhance the grounds.

The dead in this particular cemetery fulfill a valuable civic function, a function calculated in 1888 by owners of the Santa Monica Land and Water Company, a function more than to simply remind one of wars and the necessity of vigilance for the

maintenance of democracy. The permanent inertia of the dead lends the land a commodity available almost nowhere else in Los Angeles: *undevelopability*.

Los Angeles National Cemetery, by default, pulls great municipal weight through its sheer inertia in two specific channels. First, it helps maintain nearby land values; its de facto undevelopability implicitly inflates the value of all land nearby. Second, it further serves as a physical buffer for Brentwood from the relative brashness of Beverly Hills, Westwood, the Miracle Mile and the 405 freeway.

Angelenos with whom one passes the cemetery invariably gaze wistfully and say, "Can you *believe* how valuable that land must be?"

*   *   *

August 4 has been a hot day. The First Federal time/temperature clock on San Vicente had read 85 degrees at one point. One looks at the forever parched, under-tree-ed graveyard and thinks of water. One remembers the floods of the Mississippi in the summer of 1993, when water stole the river's banks, of stories of whole graveyards vanishing, their coffins dislodged like baby teeth inside the muck of a dissolving Hershey bar, of coffins landing days, weeks later on the front lawns of strangers a hundred miles away.

One thinks of Los Angeles as a city having a bad dream, dreaming of an earthquake so powerful, so violent, that the coffins of the war dead are coughed from the soil like large chunks of unswallowable meat.

Inertia will lose; dynamism will win. And suddenly the land breathes and begins to grow houses, mini-malls and roads.

*   *   *

In the end, it was *the freeway* that captured the world's imagination, not the players, so much (though they were good), or even the play, as old as the hills.

It was the *capture of the freeway* that captured the global imagination, Simpson's profound and superb monopolization of the Los Angeles freeway system. Around the world it is Los Angeles we think of when we think of freeways. And when its freeways are sick or damaged by earthquakes, we mourn for Los Angeles.

*   *   *

In a vacuum, the only possible recourse is to become a part of the vacuum: the Nembutals on the bedside table; the Magnum .457 held underneath the chin driving along the San Diego Freeway; the Menendezes shopping for Rolexes before the blood had even dried.

With a hindsight look at Brentwood, it seems inevitable that what happened did happen, if not with O.J. then with some other cataclysm reconfigured. Brentwood's is a landscape where too many unraveling and overpowering factors collide; it is a municipal and psychic bevatron, a smashing together of fame and paranoia and desire and bodies and money and power, and race and denial and media overload and all of the machinery of late-twentieth-century living.

NIGHT

Around 8:00 P.M.—the time at which estimators state that Monroe began to die—the light on the bark of the lemon-scented gum tree, a eucalyptus that dominates 356 Rockingham, is pearlescent and Maxfield Parrish–like, a bark that shimmers with the promise of magic beings and gold doubloons contained within. This is a tree that was probably planted back in the mid-twenties, around the same time Monroe was born, a tree that is around the same age of Monroe had she survived.

Monroe died just past the end of what photographers call "magic hour" with its "magic light"—the end-of-day golden glow in which all skin looks vital and all colors seem hallucinatory. She died just at that point when grays and blues become indistinguishable. Today, August 4, 1994, the day that has already begun receding into memory, memory that may or may not be forgotten.

Perhaps nature builds into us and into the world a sense of amnesia, and maybe this is our saving grace as humans, our ability to seemingly forget on cue. We are blessed and cursed with an amnesia that is so large that it frightens us while it protects us both while we sleep and while we dream.

And yes we still do dream of cities where there is still no past and where the future remains entirely unwritten, of cities where there are grassy canyons and water glazed by the sun into gold, of a billion butterflies floating through a billion coral trees, of water piped in from heaven and where there are limitless gleaming wide white freeways that will lead us off into infinity.